VISIT US AT

www.syngress.

Syngress is committed to publishing high-quality books for IT Professionals and delivering those books in media and formats that fit the demands of our customers. We are also committed to extending the utility of the book you purchase via additional materials available from our Web site.

SOLUTIONS WEB SITE

To register your book, visit www.syngress.com/solutions. Once registered, you can access our solutions@syngress.com Web pages. There you will find an assortment of value-added features such as free e-booklets related to the topic of this book, URLs of related Web site, FAQs from the book, corrections, and any updates from the author(s).

ULTIMATE CDs

Our Ultimate CD product line offers our readers budget-conscious compilations of some of our best-selling backlist titles in Adobe PDF form. These CDs are the perfect way to extend your reference library on key topics pertaining to your area of expertise, including Cisco Engineering, Microsoft Windows System Administration, CyberCrime Investigation, Open Source Security, and Firewall Configuration, to name a few.

DOWNLOADABLE EBOOKS

For readers who can't wait for hard copy, we offer most of our titles in downloadable Adobe PDF form. These eBooks are often available weeks before hard copies, and are priced affordably.

SYNGRESS OUTLET

Our outlet store at syngress.com features overstocked, out-of-print, or slightly hurt books at significant savings.

SITE LICENSING

Syngress has a well-established program for site licensing our ebooks onto servers in corporations, educational institutions, and large organizations. Contact us at sales@syngress.com for more information.

CUSTOM PUBLISHING

Many organizations welcome the ability to combine parts of multiple Syngress books, as well as their own content, into a single volume for their own internal use. Contact us at sales@syngress.com for more information.

SYNGRESS®

SYNGRESS®

Dictionary of Information Security

Robert Slade

KEY	SERIAL NUMBER
001	HJIRTCV764
002	PO9873D5FG
003	829KM8NJH2
004	5678YG7PMC
005	CVPLQ6WQ23
006	VBP965T5T5
007	HJJJ863WD3E
008	2987GVTWMK
009	629MP5SDJT
010	IMWQ295T6T

PUBLISHED BY
Syngress Publishing, Inc.
800 Hingham Street
Rockland, MA 02370

Dictionary of Information Security

Printed and bound in the United Kingdom
Transferred to Digital Print 2011
ISBN: 1597491152

Publisher: Andrew Williams   Page Layout and Art: Patricia Lupien
Cover Designer: Michael Kavish

Distributed by O'Reilly Media, Inc. in the United States and Canada.
For information on rights, translations, and bulk sales, contact Matt Pedersen, Director of Sales and Rights, at Syngress Publishing; email matt@syngress.com or fax to 781-681-3585.

Acknowledgments

Syngress would like to acknowledge the following people for their kindness and support in making this book possible.

Syngress books are now distributed in the United States and Canada by O'Reilly Media, Inc. The enthusiasm and work ethic at O'Reilly are incredible, and we would like to thank everyone there for their time and efforts to bring Syngress books to market: Tim O'Reilly, Laura Baldwin, Mark Brokering, Mike Leonard, Donna Selenko, Bonnie Sheehan, Cindy Davis, Grant Kikkert, Opol Matsutaro, Steve Hazelwood, Mark Wilson, Rick Brown, Tim Hinton, Kyle Hart, Sara Winge, Peter Pardo, Leslie Crandell, Regina Aggio Wilkinson, Pascal Honscher, Preston Paull, Susan Thompson, Bruce Stewart, Laura Schmier, Sue Willing, Mark Jacobsen, Betsy Waliszewski, Kathryn Barrett, John Chodacki, Rob Bullington, Kerry Beck, Karen Montgomery, and Patrick Dirden.

The incredibly hardworking team at Elsevier Science, including Jonathan Bunkell, Ian Seager, Duncan Enright, David Burton, Rosanna Ramacciotti, Robert Fairbrother, Miguel Sanchez, Klaus Beran, Emma Wyatt, Krista Leppiko, Marcel Koppes, Judy Chappell, Radek Janousek, Rosie Moss, David Lockley, Nicola Haden, Bill Kennedy, Martina Morris, Kai Wuerfl-Davidek, Christiane Leipersberger, Yvonne Grueneklee, Nadia Balavoine, and Chris Reinders for making certain that our vision remains worldwide in scope.

David Buckland, Marie Chieng, Lucy Chong, Leslie Lim, Audrey Gan, Pang Ai Hua, Joseph Chan, June Lim, and Siti Zuraidah Ahmad of Pansing Distributors for the enthusiasm with which they receive our books.

David Scott, Tricia Wilden, Marilla Burgess, Annette Scott, Andrew Swaffer, Stephen O'Donoghue, Bec Lowe, Mark Langley, and Anyo Geddes of Woodslane for distributing our books throughout Australia, New Zealand, Papua New Guinea, Fiji, Tonga, Solomon Islands, and the Cook Islands.

To George Raymond Slade
January 23, 1925 to January 25, 2005
who instilled in me the need for terminological exactitude

About the Author

Rob Slade is a data communications, information security, and management consultant from North Vancouver, British Columbia, Canada. His first love is teaching (before research turned him into a virus expert), and he got into computers because of an interest in what they could do to improve the education process in the public school system. He holds a B.Sc. from the University of British Columbia, an M.S. (in Computer and Information Science Education) from the University of Oregon, and a Diploma of Christian Studies from Regent College.

Rob has formal training in data communications and exploration with the online community, and has done communications training for a number of international commercial seminar firms. His technical jobs have involved everything from support of terminal emulation programs to satellite communications. In concert with his background in education, he prepared the technical and interface side of the World LOGO Conference, the first time an on–site conference was fully linked to online participants.

His research into computer viral programs started when they first appeared as a major problem "in the wild." Acting initially as the unofficial archivist for the budding research community, he became known for "Mr. Slade's lists" of virus information. While part of the working group for the VIRUS-L FAQ, he was best known for a series of review and tutorial articles that were eventually published as *Robert Slade's Guide to Computer Viruses*. In an attempt to update this material, he coauthored *Viruses Revealed*. As an outgrowth of the virus research, he prepared the world's first course on forensic programming, which became the first book on *Software Forensics*. As a

Senior Instructor for (ISC)^2, Rob has been working on a glossary of security terms (which became this book) and references for CISSP candidate students, describing the various CISSP study guides and recommended resources for the different domains. He is also working on the Community Security Education project, attempting to promote security awareness for the general public as a means of reducing overall information security threats.

Despite all of this work, Rob is best known for gleefully (and regularly) reviewing technical books, producing reviews that appear on appropriate newsgroups and mailing lists, including groups and lists related to the topics of the individual titles—pointing out the errors in literally thousands of books written by other people is easier and more fun than writing real stuff. More information than anyone would want to know about him is available at http://victoria.tc.ca/techrev/rms.htm. It is next to impossible to get him to take "bio" writing seriously.

Forewords

Fred Cohen is best known as the inventor of computer virus defense techniques, the principal investigator whose team defined the information assurance problem as it relates to critical infrastructure protection today, as a seminal researcher in the use of deception for information protection, and as a topflight information protection consultant. But his work on information protection extends far beyond these areas. In the 1970s he designed network protocols for secure digital networks carrying voice, video, and data; and he helped develop and prototype the electronic cashwatch for implementing personal digital money

systems. In the 1980s, he developed integrity mechanisms for secure operating systems, consulted for many major corporations, taught short courses in information protection to over 10,000 students worldwide, and in 1989, he won the prestigious international Information Technology Award for his work on integrity protection.

In the 1990s, he developed protection testing and audit techniques and systems, secure Internet servers and systems, defensive information warfare techniques and systems, early systems using deception for information protection, and bootable CDs designed for forensics and secure server applications. All told, the protection techniques he pioneered now help to defend more than three quarters of all the computers in the world.

Fred has authored almost 200 invited, refereed, and other scientific and management research articles, writes a monthly column for *Network Security* magazine on managing network security, and has written several widely read books on information protection. His series of "Infosec Baseline" studies have been widely used by the research community as stepping off points for further research, his "50 Ways" series is very popular among practitioners looking for issues to be addressed, and his most recent "Protection for Deception" series of papers is widely cited.

As a corporate consultant Fred has helped secure some of the world's largest companies in the fields of information technology, microelectronics, pharmaceuticals, manufacturing, transportation, telecommunications, and the financial and information industries. As a consultant to and researcher for the U.S. government, he was the principal investigator on seminal studies in defensive information operations. He was the principal investigator on the national information security technical baseline series of reports, founded the College Cyber Defenders program at Sandia National Laboratories that ultimately led to the formation of the CyberCorps program, and led projects

ranging from "Resilience" to "The Invisible Router." He has also worked in critical infrastructure protection, with law enforcement, and with the intelligence community to help improve their ability to deal with computer-related crime and emerging threats to national security. He has worked on issues of digital forensics, including work for many large corporations and pro bono and state-funded work for indigent defendants, and in 2002, won the "Techno-Security Industry Professional of the Year" Award.

Fred has participated in and created numerous strategic scenario games. He devised and ran the first Internet-based strategic information warfare wargame and held several initial trial Internet-based games involving national defense and corporate personnel. In 1998, he introduced the *Internet Game* for information security policy development, training, and awareness in corporate, educational, and government environments, and followed this up with the *Sexual Harassment Game,* which helps train employees on sexual harassment policies and processes. His recent introduction of several security games and simulations to the Internet are excellent examples of the work he has done in this area. He has also developed several strategic scenarios for government and private use.

Over the past 25 years, Fred has managed organizations and projects with as many as 250 employees. Several projects he led have resulted in new business in excess of $10 million, and one project led to a five-year government contract with a ceiling of over $1.7 billion. He led a 35-person research team at Sandia National Laboratories for almost five years and produced several patents, copyrighted software programs, and publications in the process.

His combination of management, technical, and communication skills allows him to effectively bridge the gap between decision makers and implementers. His involvement in and understanding of corporate, national, and global issues provides a context that allows him to meet

challenges of unlimited size and scope. With more than 25 years of experience and a global reputation for integrity, accuracy, and innovation, Fred Cohen is widely considered one of the world's leading authorities in information protection.

Jack Holleran has had an interesting career pretending to be a college professor (adjunct at Anne Arundel Community College, graduate adjunct at Towson University and Johns Hopkins University), umpire (baseball, softball), commercial instructor (ISC2), Information Assurance Engineer (Engineering Solutions, Inc.), Chairman (various roles: National Information Systems Security Conference, Black Hat, DefCon, and GovSec), and Technical Director (retired, National Computer Security Center, National Security Agency). When he isn't pretending to work, he is the happy grandfather of three, and hopes to break Rob's record of four. Jack graduated from Duquesne University (B.S.) and Central Michigan University (M.A.) with postgraduate work in Computer Science at the University of Maryland.

Peter G. Neumann has doctorates from Harvard and Darmstadt. After 10 years at Bell Labs in Murray Hill, NJ, in the 1960s, during which he was heavily involved in the Multics development jointly with MIT and Honeywell, he has been in SRI's Computer Science Lab since September 1971. He is concerned with computer systems and networks, trustworthiness/dependability, high assurance, security, reliability, survivability, safety, and many risk-related issues such as voting system integrity, crypto policy, social implications, and human needs, including privacy. He moderates the ACM Risks Forum, edits CACM's monthly *Inside Risks* column, chairs the ACM Committee on Computers and Public Policy, and chairs the National

Committee for Voting Integrity (www.epic.org/ privacy/voting). He created ACM SIGSOFT's *Software Engineering Notes* in 1976, was its editor for 19 years, and still contributes the RISKS section. He cofounded People For Internet Responsibility (PFIR, www.PFIR.org). His 1995 book, *Computer-Related Risks,* is still timely! He is a Fellow of the ACM, IEEE, and AAAS, and an SRI Fellow. He received the National Computer System Security Award in 2002 and the ACM SIGSAC Outstanding Contributions Award in 2005. He is a member of the U.S. Government Accountability Office Executive Council on Information Management and Technology, and the California Office of Privacy Protection advisory council. He has taught courses at Darmstadt, Stanford, U.C. Berkeley, and the University of Maryland. See his Web site (www.csl.sri.com/neumann) for further background, Senate and House testimonies, papers, bibliography, and so forth.

Hal Tipton, currently an independent consultant and past president of the International Information System Security Certification Consortium, was Director of Computer Security for Rockwell International Corporation for about 15 years. He initiated the Rockwell computer and data security program in 1977 and continued to administer, develop, enhance, and expand the program to accommodate the control needs produced by technological advances until his retirement from Rockwell in 1994.

He has been a member of the Information Systems Security Association (ISSA) since 1982, was president of the Los Angeles Chapter in 1984, and president of the national organization of ISSA (1987–1989). He was added to the ISSA Hall of Fame and the ISSA Honor Role in 2000. He was a member of the National Institute for Standards and Technology (NIST) Computer and

Telecommunications Security Council, and the National Research Council Secure Systems Study Committee (for the National Academy of Science). He holds a B.S. in Engineering from the U.S. Naval Academy, an M.A. in Personnel Administration from George Washington University, and a Certificate in Computer Science from the University of California at Irvine. He is a Certified Information System Security Professional (CISSP), ISSAP, and ISSMP.

He has been a speaker at all the major information security conferences, including Computer Security Institute, the ISSA Annual Working Conference, the Computer Security Workshop, MIS Conferences, AIS Security for Space Operations, DOE Computer Security Conference, National Computer Security Conference, IIA Security Conference, EDPAA, UCCEL Security & Audit Users Conference, and Industrial Security Awareness Conference.

He has conducted/participated in information security seminars for (ISC)^2, Frost & Sullivan, UCI, CSULB, System Exchange Seminars, and the Institute for International Research. He received the Computer Security Institute "Lifetime Achievement Award" in 1994 and the (ISC)^2 "Hal Tipton Award" in 2001.

Dr. Eugene Spafford is a professor with a joint appointment in Computer Sciences and Electrical and Computer Engineering at Purdue University, where he has served on the faculty since 1987. He is also a professor of philosophy (courtesy) and a professor of communication (courtesy). He serves on a number of advisory and editorial boards, and is internationally known for his writing, research, and speaking on issues of security and ethics. Currently, Spaf (as he is known to his friends, colleagues, and students) has research interests primarily in the areas of information security, computer crime investigation, and information ethics.

Spaf is Executive Director of the Purdue CERIAS (Center for Education and Research in Information Assurance and Security) and was the founder and director of the (superseded) COAST Laboratory.

Spaf is also involved in a number of professional societies and activities outside Purdue, including serving on the Board of Directors of the Computing Research Association and as chair of the Association of Computing Machinery's (ACM's) US Public Policy Committee. He was a member of the President's Information Technology Advisory Committee (PITAC) in 2003-2005, and continues to serve as an adviser to over a dozen federal agencies and major corporations.

Spaf received his B.A. degree with a double major in mathematics and computer sciences from the State University College at Brockport (1979, NY). Upon graduation, he was honored with a SUNY College President's Citation. He then attended the School of Information and Computer Sciences (now the College of Computing) at the Georgia Institute of Technology, holding both a Georgia Tech President's Fellowship and a National Science Foundation Graduate Fellowship. He received his M.S. in 1981 and his Ph.D. in 1986 for his design and implementation of the original Clouds reliable, distributed operating system kernel, and for his contributions as one of the original members of the Clouds design team.

Author
Acknowledgments

Carole McClendon of Waterside Productions, my agent, put up with this project, and me, for many years before it finally saw print.

Hal Tipton, whose contributions to both security education and security literature are too numerous to mention, allowed me to join "the best instructor corps in the world," which gave rise to this whole thing. The CISSP CBK instructors themselves have been active in promoting the glossary, and in feeding back errors and omissions. I look forward to seeing you all again at the next T3.

Gary and Mae Shearman are the powers behind the Victoria TelecommunityNet. They have, for many years, provided a home for the online glossary, study resources, and book reviews, despite my highly irregular updating schedule.

A sincere thank you to my forewarders, who, though extremely busy, all graciously responded to an emergency request, at the last minute, when the contract (with a short deadline) arrived while I was teaching out of town. Each contributed an important perspective to the project (and even specific suggestions for additions and corrections).

My thanks to Amorette Pedersen, Co-Founder of Syngress Publishing, for agreeing that the Oxford English Dictionary is a valid lexical reference, and for sticking to her commitments in the face of intransigent copy editors.

Gloria, my copy editor, developmental editor, living style sheet, fellow player with words, best friend, organizer of outings with grandchildren, and wife, again checked over this manuscript, this time interpreting HTML, doing it on a laptop, and doing it all in a week.

Any remaining errors are due to my stubbornness in not taking her advice.

Preface

Why a dictionary?

When I was allowed to join the august ranks of those facilitating the (ISC)² (International Information Systems Security Certification Consortium) CISSP (Certified Information Systems Security Professional) CBK (Common Body of Knowledge) review seminar, one thing quickly became very clear: the desperate need for a dictionary. All fields of technology have their own jargon. Those of us in security tend to be worse than those in other fields, because we frequently take perfectly good words or phrases and invest them with specialized meanings.

In fact, one of the CISSP study guides, the *CISSP (Exam Cram)* by Mandy Andress, is essentially a glossary. It is in topical, and not alphabetical, order, but is presented as a list of key terms and phrases.

This need for a better explanation of the mass of security terminology was rather ironic in regard to the CISSP seminars. The CISSP certification is described in a number of ways. While some security professionals are generalists and others specialize in diverse fields, we try to stress to candidates that one of the benefits of a CISSP designation is that it ensures that the holder knows what he (or she) is talking about in regard to security. All CISSPs should, at the very least, be able to talk to each other. (Actually, I've seen this work out in rather dramatic ways at times.)

Hadn't someone already done that?

There are, and were, other security glossaries. RFC 2828 (available at www.ietf.org/rfc/rfc2828.txt), the *Internet Security Glossary* is a complete and careful work intended to outline security-related terms that should (and some that should not) be used in Internet Standards Documents (ISDs). I recommend it for those interested in network security, but, of course, it doesn't touch on other security domains.

Corey Schou's *Draft Comprehensive Information Assurance Dictionary* (http://security.isu.edu/pdf/NIATECV30d.pdf) is a comprehensive document, the result of an enormous amount of work to determine the origin of various terms. However, it includes a great deal of material that has no specific relation to information security, save that it deals with computers or other technology. It is also a wonderful source of technology history trivia. Unfortunately, it's a bit hefty for those who simply want to look up a specific security term.

Governments, particularly the United States government and military, have a big jump on the rest of us with regard to security. A source for government material is the *National Information Systems Security (INFOSEC) Glossary* (www.cultural.com/web/security/infosec.glossary.html), which dates from 1992. Unfortunately, the military got to be a bit too specialized, and a number of these terms are used nowhere else.

Two groups involved in security have developed glossaries: SANS (Sysadmin, Audit, Network, Security) at www.sans.org/resources/glossary.php, and ISACA (the Information Systems Audit and Control Association) at www.isaca.org/glossary.htm. They tend to provide the bare minimum in terms of information and the number of entries.

Some vendors have also created glossaries: AuditMyPC at www.auditmypc.com/freescan/glossary.asp, and ANNA Ltd. at www.softsecurity.com/doc/glossary_sec.html. These are even smaller.

So, it seems there is still a need for a dictionary that covers all the basic jargon of security, without bloating itself with every minor variation on a terminological theme. I put together a glossary on a Web page (http://victoria.tc.ca/techrev/ secgloss.htm, through the kind offices of Victoria TelecommunityNet), and set about making it more complete. (Now that this book is finally in print, the full dictionary has been removed, but a page with errata and updates will still be there.)

After I had put together the glossary on the Web, a couple of printed security dictionaries were published. The first was the *Internet Security Dictionary* by Vir V. Phoha. This was a valuable addition to the security bookshelf, as the only printed reference, but of the 1,400 terms defined in the book, a number are simply minor variations on a theme. (There are, for example, 12 phrases beginning with "access.") Much of the material is based on the old United States military terminology. Some new and slang terms have been included, but some of these entries are only very vaguely related to security. Definitions tend to be terse, and many lack necessary detail.

A couple of years later, Urs Gattiker published *The Information Security Dictionary*. However, it is incomplete, contains a number of errors of fact, and many of the entries are inconsistent with other published security literature.

OK, but why me?

In regard to putting together a dictionary, I had a head start. My background in security was in malware research, and those of us in the antivirus community tend to make up a lot of specialized terms as well. I had included a fairly extensive glossary in my first book, and I'd just finished adding a bunch more entries for my second. So I already had a core set of terms, albeit in one particular field.

I'm also "the book guy." I review a lot of the security literature, and one of things I see is that the meaning of words tends to drift over time. Therefore, I have an advantage in knowing which words are currently being used, which ones are being replaced by others, and which were silly to begin with and should never have been used in the first place.

I have also reviewed a number of dictionaries over the years. There are a great many in the telecommunications field; they used to be given away as freebies by vendors at trade shows. There are so many on the market that when I was reviewing books for a telecommunications magazine some years back, every year we had a special "dictionaries" column.

Who's going to read a dictionary?

I assume that the largest single audience for this book will be students, of one type or another. You may be going for the CISSP exam. (For most of its life, the Web version was being used as a resource for CISSP candidates.) You may be writing another security certification. You may be a student in a computer security program in a college or university. Or, you may simply be a lifelong learner.

Then there are the security professionals. Nobody is an expert in all the fields of security, so here is a reference to those areas in which you have not worked. Finally, you'll get to know what your colleagues down the hall have been talking about all these years. (You'll also be one of the people who "get" most of the jokes.)

How about the system and network administrators? Even if your job isn't specifically about security, you have to deal with it these days as a matter of course. So, you need to know what the latest vulnerability advisories are discussing, and possibly what makes a proxy firewall different from a packet filter.

Managers, of course, have to address risk management whether their jobs relate to security or not. But if you have special responsibilities for security, even if you have specialists and professionals who do the hands-on work for you, you need to know what they are talking about, what the vendors are talking about when they are trying to sell you something, and whether what either group is saying actually means anything.

What is this dictionary like?

Dictionaries are usually rather formal in tone. I have deliberately tried to break that pattern. Formal definitions do exist in these pages, but, where a term carries an important concept, I have tried to speak plainly. I'm sure some readers will consider a number of the entries flippant; hopefully, I haven't introduced too many errors in my wording. (Fred, in his Foreword, found the fractionally fanciful flavour of this folio.)

(I have not yet succeeded in completely breaking away from a formal tone. As I am finishing the manuscript for the dictionary, I am also reviewing "Information Security and Employee Behaviour," by Angus McIlwraith. He makes the point that we in security tend to use a lot of complicated words with Latinate roots, even where perfectly acceptable simple alternatives exist. Reading his examples, I cringe, recognizing stuff I haven't fixed yet. Too late for this edition, I guess, but I suppose I know what my first job will be once this manuscript finally gets shipped off to the printer.) (By the way, I recommend McIlwraith's book.)

This glossary concentrates on usage of terms. Capitalization and spelling generally follow the most common usage, except where such usage can be shown to be based on a specific error. Acronyms and phrases have the definition placed with the most commonly used form; for example, in most cases the phrase "denial of service" is used unless it has been previously defined in an article as the acronym "DoS," whereas the acronym "DDoS" is almost universally used in preference to the phrase "distributed denial of service." In all cases, an attempt has been made to have a link from the lesser used form to the definition.

I have not tried to be exhaustive in listing every variation on a theme. Therefore, when a term is listed in bold font, indicating a link to another entry, there may be a slight variation. If, for example, you see "sanity checking" printed in italics in one definition, the related entry might be "sanity check."

There are many security terms that are local. For example, a large amount of security literature produced in the United States makes reference to United States Department of Defense materials that were not picked up by the security community, or to U.S. legislation that has no relevance in other countries. When such material is included here, I have tried to make note of its origin in the definition.

Those who are serious about dictionaries as dictionaries will find this one lacking. I have not included pronunciation, and in most cases, I have no information about the origin and derivation of terms. I have concentrated on security students and professionals; those researching the history of technical language will probably not find what they are looking for here.

Actually, it's hard to say whether this is a dictionary or an encyclopedia. At times, I have felt that a simple definition isn't good enough, and have expanded some terms at length. Indeed, some of the material in this book is subjective and opinionated. (So am I.) I know that many are going to disagree in places. However, I know that a great many people need to come up to speed in many areas of security, and need more than definitions that use a lot of words that have, themselves, to be defined. The choice of how to do this is subjective. If you disagree with a decision I've made, then contact me, and hopefully we can make the next edition better.

This work is very much "in process." There are lots of candidates for the fastest changing area of technology, but I think security has a lock on the top spot. Whatever else develops in any area of technology tends to have implications for security. Therefore, I expect that there will be editions of this dictionary to come, in years to come, with new and updated terms. Please report any errors or omissions to slade@victoria.tc.ca or rslade@computercrime.org. I also set up a mailing list for those who want to be more involved with the project: you can join at secgloss-subscribe@egroups.com.

Foreword by Gene Spafford, Purdue University

Science makes progress through the process of hypothesis, experiment, analysis, and description. Engineering builds on scientific results. To clearly convey those results and establish a common frame of reference requires clarity, precision, and agreed-upon language. Mathematics provides one such system of communication, but it doesn't convey everything we might wish to express. It is left to human language to express concepts and relationships fundamental to our shared progress.

Computing is a discipline that has matured over the last half-century as a new field of science and engineering. Within that discipline, we have witnessed the emergence of new specializations, each with its own particular constructs, terms, ground truths, formalisms, and challenges. One specialization, addressing misuse of computing resources, spans many of those other disciplines yet retains its own special character. Whether referred to as cyber security, information security, information assurance, or one of several other terms, the core holds great challenges and importance to everyone working in computing... and everyone affected by computers. As such, having a common lexicon to use when talking about the area is of growing importance.

Rob Slade has been involved in information security as an author, researcher, and reviewer for many years. In that time, he has surveyed most of the literature, and contributed several important components to it. From that broad experience, he has compiled this glossary of infosec-related terms. Although not everyone will completely agree with every entry, it provides a valuable first pass at a comprehensive set of definitions that can be used by practitioner and end user alike. Rob's glossary provides a citable, common source we can all use as we attempt to describe some of the vexing problems we face with cyber security and privacy—and their solutions.

Thank you, Rob.

Foreword by
Fred Cohen,
Security Posture,
University of New Haven

Foreword: (1) a short piece written by someone with a name to introduce and elucidate upon the positive values associated with a written work; (2) a way to get your name into someone else's book; (3) something the author asks someone else to do because it would be unseemly to write it himself; (4) something the publisher says will increase sales.

Forword: (1) a program that does forensics for Word documents; (2) a way to get a software product I used in a case once advertised surreptitiously in someone else's book; (3) something I slipped past the editors; (4) something my publisher says will increase my sales of Forword.

If a "glossary" glosses over things, then Rob Slade has a "bug" in his title. While most of us have our own definitions of words, and there are many terms of art used in the "security" field that are interpreted differently by many of us (see "hacker" or "hack" as opposed to "cracker" or "crack"), Rob has created an extensive, if not comprehensive, if not comprehensible, "disclosure" of what most in the field would find reasonably close to the way we use these terms. Which in an emerging field is a Herculean task.

While I could not "decipher" how "deception" included "decryption," I could see how "data diddling" could have corrupted the "data integrity" when a "dark-side hacker" created a "deadlock." This reminds me of a program I wrote long ago that took different kinds of keywords and automatically generated sequences of them in valid syntax to produce proposals. But that's a different story...

Just between you and me (see "confidentiality"), most of the people who use most of these words haven't bothered to make sure their usage is right (see "integrity"). Of course, "hashing" out my personal views on "users" of incorrect terminological expressions should probably be done elsewhere, lest I get a "mail storm" of "spam" from some "malicious" "evil twin" that "exploits" a "fail over" "false alarm" to "infect" a file (see "file infector") that creates a "fault" in a "filter" that "firewalls" the "flow control" that "front ends" the "freeware" used by the "fraudsters" that "format" the "spam" that I get. For that reason, I include this "disclaimer"… just kidding—as Rob was when he wrote the glossary entry for it.

As you probably have an "awareness" by now, it is hard to write a simple sentence without using one of the words Rob provides in his glossary. And for complex sentences, such as the ones I tend to write in flowery introductions such as this one, it is downright impossible to do so. Okay, that was an exception. (Actually, "exception" should be in there but isn't!) But by now, I think you get my point. If you are going to talk to anyone in "computer security" (a town in Iowa as I understand it), and you don't know most of the words in Rob's glossary, you can't "assure" that their "emanations" will be properly understood.

And from a purely practical perspective, if you want to fake being a computer security expert, you had better know the difference between the "confinement property" and the "star property."—FC

Foreword by Hal Tipton, CISSP, ISSAP, ISSMP

During the past 30 or so years, as the field of information security has grown from fledging status to an overarching giant, developers in both the private and public sectors have created thousands of tools and protocols to help ensure the confidentiality, integrity, and availability of all types of information resources. Quite naturally, the terminology and definitions of terms and concepts multiplied exponentially. Unfortunately, during this process, the same term and/or acronym described, in many cases, very different things. The state today is that we have difficulty communicating our thoughts to each other in this profession because there is no standard glossary of terms we all subscribe to and understand.

Several efforts in the past have resulted in compiling extensive terms and listing their several definitions, but have failed to solve the problem. What is needed now in the world of information security is a single glossary of terms using the preferred definition for each term to be published and used throughout the world.

I personally have come face to face with this definition problem as the Chief Instructor over the past dozen years for the International Information Systems Security Certification Consortium (ISC)². In that role, I have developed several courses that addressed topics contained in the Common Body of Knowledge for the information security field that dealt with concepts and definitions. I struggled continuously to select the most appropriate definition for many of the most important terms. As a result, I am supportive of the idea of publishing an official glossary of terms for information security professionals and related personnel.

Rob Slade has undertaken this difficult task, and his Dictionary should prove to be one of the most helpful additions to the professional library of every one of us working in the field of information security. Obviously, this first edition is only the beginning. As the field continues to expand, more and more terms will be developed that require sorting out and unique definitions. This means that the Dictionary will be a living, growing document for the foreseeable future.

Foreword by Peter G. Neumann, ACM Risks Forum Moderator

Given that there is no such thing as perfect security, we should not expect a perfect glossary—because there is always so much more to be said. However, as a first approximation, this glossary is well conceived and well executed.

Slade's knowledge of the subject matter is outstanding, as is his commitment to make this a work in progress. I suspect it will continue to evolve—perhaps even somewhat like George Washington's original axe (which has had many new handles and many new blades, but is still the same old axe).

Foreword by Jack Holleran, CISSP

Welcome to the brave new world of computer security, data security, information security, information assurance, and, more often than not, information overload. Yes, I know the field has been around since the 1960s, but we, and this field, are still evolving.

As an individual, it is extremely difficult to have cogent dialogue when a listener or reader doesn't know what values to assign to terminology. Rob's *Dictionary of Information Security* can remove many of these impediments. Rob provides a consistent, well-written reference point for students and professionals.

As teachers, professionals, and communicators, our primary goal is to present our knowledge such that our students, peers, and management can interpret, communicate, and understand the ideas as we intended. This dictionary provides the framework and boundaries for words and terminology that we can use in our professional venues.

As a CISSP, many of the terms and words we use are succinct and well defined. When we take certification exams, we will see many of these terms. Knowing their meaning can only improve our chances of selecting the right answer.

Roget[1] provides the term glossary with the synonyms lexicon, reference, terminology, and encyclopedia. Indirect synonyms include definition, explanation, interpretation, codification, and observation.

This book is all of that and more; it helps us provide a better writer-to-reader dialogue. Our time is valuable; the price of this book can be amortized in spending less time discussing definitions. This book will have a close location in my reference library!

[1] Source: *Roget's New Millennium Thesaurus*, First Edition (v 1.2.1) ©2006 by Lexico Publishing Group, LLC. All rights reserved.

Introduction

Introduction to Infosecspeak

Communities often define themselves by vocabulary that those in the inner circle know, and those on the outside do not. Security people do this as well, and sometimes more than most. We are, after all, the professionally paranoid, and it is more important to us than to most other groups to know who belongs.

This linguistic identification can backfire. Law enforcement personnel have a specific and distinctive vocabulary all their own. I have been informed by a number of members of police forces that police officers are very susceptible to social engineering, or scams, due to this fact. If you know the language, you must be "one of us."

Understanding the language of the security community is made more difficult because there are multiple security communities. Security people come from backgrounds such as the military, government, academia, industry, system administration, law enforcement, and the intelligence community. Very often, these groups don't talk to each other.

In terms of the security lexicon, the first contribution has to be the government and military, particularly from the United States. A number of terms arose from the language developed in that arena, and the formal studies funded from that source. Several of those definitions are included here. Usage has fallen off, in the face of new technologies and use, but they may be of historical interest, and still have force in security literature overall.

The Internet and networking technologies have become major factors in security. While the older security functions and concepts are still valid, they are increasingly impacted by network activities.

Therefore, a number of the terms included here relate to communications. I have tried to reduce the number of these items to those closely associated with security protection or attacks.

There are different cultures involved in the technical world. One of the best examinations of technical culture in general is the introduction to the "Jargon File." (Do a Web search on that term: you'll find lots of copies around the world.)

It is interesting to look at the flow of linguistic practices through these cultures. Abstract Syntax Notation (ASN.1) begat various network protocols, which influenced those developing object-oriented programming languages, which inspired those working in multimedia, and the bias popped out in consumer products. You think I exaggerate?

Variables, and other naming conventions, in ASN.1 run words together, separating them by capitalizing the initial letter of each word, but not the first. So what is the hot new technology on the market right now? The iPod, which is an Internet (loaded) Pod (for holding music).

(The contraction of Internet to a simple "i" is related to another technical culture artifact: the tendency, particularly when using email or other text-based message systems, to reduce typing as much as possible, and go for acronyms.)

Some phrases in security seem to be chosen strictly for their contrary nature. You will note that occasional English words are taken and the spelling deliberately modified. Other factors seem to be a tendency toward aggressive language, as befitting a culture that sees adversaries on every network link, and dangers at every turn. Security people also tend to feel embattled and isolated, even from those with whom they are working. Therefore, you will notice a tendency toward pomposity, likely in an attempt to promote self-importance (and possibly even self-esteem).

The terms included here have been culled from a variety of sources over a long period of time. The reader will note that I have sometimes suggested that a specific entry should not be used. I have included these items to give the student or professional a reference. The objective, however, should be to ensure that your own communications are as clear as possible.

Symbols

*-property *Bell-La Padula* security model rule allowing a
subject write access to an *object* only if the security
level of the object is higher than, or dominates, the
security level of the subject. In other words, you can
only tell something to someone whose clearance is
equal to or higher than yours is. Pronounced, and
sometimes written, star property. Also called confinement property. There is a related *strong star property* in database security.

Numbers

3DES see *triple DES*

A

ABA Guidelines American Bar Association (ABA) Digital Signature Guidelines, a framework of legal principles for using *digital signatures* and digital certificates in electronic commerce

ABEND abnormal termination of a software process or a system (ABnormal END); a crash. The word derives from an error message originally displayed on the IBM 360 computer: it does not appear in error messages of current operating systems although the term is still used. Abnormal or unexpected termination may result in possible security vulnerabilities, and so the term may also be used to refer to the option to terminate, in a controlled manner, a processing activity in a computer system because it is impossible or undesirable for the activity to proceed.

Abstract Syntax Notation One (ASN.1) standard for describing data *objects*, this notation format is important to security because of its significance in networking discussions. OSI (Open System Interconnection) standards use ASN.1 to specify data formats for protocols. Syntax is needed to define abstract objects, and encoding rules are needed to transform between abstract objects and bit strings. In ASN.1, formal names are written without spaces, and separate words in a name are indicated by capitalizing the first letter of each word except the first word. For example, the name of a CRL is "certificateRevocationList."

Acceptable Use Policy (AUP) written policy outlining the usage that may or may not be made of computing or network resources. Previously, this applied primarily to institutions (such as universities) providing access to systems such as the Internet. Although the term is currently not as widely used, these instructions should still be part of a company's *security policy*.

acceptance inspection the final inspection to determine whether a facility or system meets the specified technical and performance standards. Similar to *certification* although generally referring to facilities rather than applications. This inspection is held immediately following facility and software testing and is the basis for commissioning or accepting the information system. If the system is accepted, it receives *accreditation*.

access ability and means to communicate with or otherwise interact with a system: a specific type of interaction between a *subject* and an *object* that results in the flow of information from one to the other. A subject may access a file object to obtain data, or a subject may access a system resource and give it command information to obtain service. There is not full agreement on the definition of access: some would insist that the simple ability to receive information is not access unless the subject can also command the object.

access control process of limiting access to the resources of a system only to authorized users, programs, processes, or other systems (in a network).

Synonymous with controlled access and limited access. Access control may be an administrative, physical, or technical *control*, but is most commonly implemented via technical controls limiting access to information or resources on a system. Access control is generally a preventive control.

access control list list of users, programs, and/or processes and the specifications of access categories to which each is assigned

access control mechanism hardware or software features, operating procedures, management procedures, and various combinations of these designed to detect and prevent unauthorized access and to permit authorized access in an automated system. Access control lists are a technical access control mechanism.

access level the hierarchical portion of the security level used to identify the sensitivity of data and the clearance or *authorization* of users. Note: The access level, in conjunction with the non-hierarchical categories, forms the *sensitivity label* of an *object*. See *category*, *security level*, and *sensitivity label*.

access period segment of time, generally expressed on a daily or weekly basis, during which access rights prevail

access type the nature of an access right to a particular device, program, or file (e.g., read, write, execute, append, modify, delete, or create)

accountability in the narrow view of technical security, the property that enables activities on a system to be traced to individuals (or entities) who may then be held responsible for their actions. More broadly, when dealing with ethics, the duty or voluntary agreement to be responsible for one's actions, particularly with regard to visibility, transparency, or explanation. In this latter sense, to be accountable, one may have to freely reduce one's claim on certain other properties that are ordinarily considered part of security, such as *privacy*.

accreditation formal declaration by the command or management authority that the system is approved to operate in a particular security mode using a prescribed set of *safeguards*. Accreditation is the official management authorization for operation of a system and is based on the *certification* process and other management considerations. The accreditation statement affixes security responsibility with the management or operating authority, and shows that due care has been taken for security. Essentially, accreditation involves acceptance of the system.

accreditation authority management or command level with authority to accept a particular system

activation in *business continuity planning*, the implementation of a procedure, activity, or plan in response to an *event* or *incident*

active *attack* or *exploit* involving an attempt to change or influence a system. See also *passive*, which generally involves listening or spying.

active response the system automatically blocks or acts against the progress of a detected attack. The response may take one of three forms: amending the environment (such as changing entries in firewall tables), collecting more information, or striking back against the user. (The last option is not recommended.)

ActiveX ActiveX controls are software modules based on Microsoft's Component Object Model (COM) architecture and appear to be Microsoft's preferred form of active content for Web pages. ActiveX controls are, in fact, almost identical in structure to MS Windows programs, and have full system access. The only security provision is a *digital signature* system called *Authenticode*, which offers only "run/don't run" options, and has additional security limitations.

activity monitor type of antiviral software that checks for signs of suspicious activity, such as attempts to rewrite program files, format disks, etc. The term *activity monitor* is usually considered to include *operation restrictor* type software (also known as activity blocker or behaviour blocker), but is sometimes differentiated in that an activity monitor may just alert the operator to the attempt, rather than disabling it.

activity blocker see *operation restrictor*

add-on security the retrofitting of protection mechanisms, implemented by hardware or software

administrative control see *controls*

administrative security the management constraints and supplemental controls established to provide an acceptable level of protection for data. Synonymous with *procedural security*. More commonly referred to as *administrative controls*.

Advanced Encryption Standard (AES) standard developed by the United States National Institute of Standards and Technology to succeed *DES*. Intended to specify an unclassified, publicly disclosed, *symmetric encryption* algorithm, available royalty-free worldwide.

adversary entity that *attacks*, or is a *threat* to, a system

adware while not necessarily *malware*, adware is considered to go beyond the reasonable advertising one might expect from *freeware* or *shareware*. Typically, a separate program that is installed at the same time as a shareware or similar program, adware will usually continue to generate advertising even when the user is not running the originally desired program. See also *cookies*, *spyware*, and *web bugs*.

aggregation circumstance in which higher level information (which may be thought to be subject to a higher level of security clearance) may be inferred from a large number of lower level data items. As a result, a collection of information items may require classification at a higher security level than any of the individual items that comprise it.

aggregation problem occurrence when a subject's right to individual pieces of information results in knowledge to which the subject does not have a right. This is usually addressed by restricting combinations of accesses in certain ways.

AH see *Authentication Header*

airplane rule complexity increases the possibility of failure; conversely, simplicity increases robustness. The name comes from the observation that, while it appears obvious that having more than one engine in an airplane increases safety, in fact, a twin-engine airplane has twice as many engine problems as a single-engine airplane, and the loss of either engine may lead to instability.

AIS Automated Information System. Term formerly used by the United States government and military for computer or electronic information systems. Sometimes found in older security texts.

alarm any of a number of devices having three basic components: a sensor (that determines or triggers on some condition), a communications or control system, and an actuator or annunciator (that takes some action or alerts a user or operator). Alarms come in a wide variety of forms and complexities. Antiviral software may have a scanning engine (sensor), user interface (control), and report screen (annunciator). CCTV (Closed Circuit TeleVision) systems may have cameras (sensor), circuit (communications), and monitors (annunciator). Simple fire sprinkler heads have all components in one package: a plug that melts at high temperature (sensor) unblocking the flow (control) of the water behind it (actuator).

alert notification that an *event* or *incident* has occurred

alert phase initial phase of a *business continuity* or *disaster recovery* plan, during which the first emergency actions, and assessments of damage and implications, take place

algorithm sequence of steps needed to solve logical or mathematical problems. In security, the term usually refers to *cryptographic algorithms* used in *encryption* or *decryption* of data files and messages and to create *digital signatures*, but it may also refer to pattern matching in virus or *intrusion* detection that does not rely on the use of a simple scan string (see *signature*).

alias name that an entity uses in place of its real name, in computing usually for purposes of convenience or brevity, but in security often for the purpose of either *anonymity* or deception

alternate routing routing of a call or message over a substitute route when a primary route is unavailable for immediate use. Note that while this function increases *availability*, it may create problems with *integrity* or possibly *confidentiality*.

alternate site site pre-arranged for use in the event of a *business continuity incident*. See *cold site*, *warm site*, and *hot site*.

annual loss expectancy (ALE) the expected yearly dollar value loss from the system or activity by attacks or threats. Generally calculated by taking the value of a single such loss by a given threat or event (single loss expectancy), and multiplying by the expected number of events over time (annual rate of occurrence) (therefore also known as annualized loss expectancy). Also, sometimes the sum of a number of such calculations.

anomaly detection detecting intrusions by looking for activity that is different from the user's or system's normal behaviour. A type of *intrusion detection system*.

anonymous the condition of having an identity that is unknown or concealed. To hide an entity's real name, an *alias* may be used. In some applications, anonymous entities may be completely untraceable. See also *anonymous login*.

anonymous login *access control* feature (or weakness) in many Internet hosts that enables users to gain access to general-purpose or public services and resources on a host (such as allowing any user to transfer data using *ftp*) without having a pre-established, user-specific account (i.e., username and secret password). This feature exposes a system to more threats than when all the users are known, pre-registered entities who are individually *accountable* for their actions.

ANSI bomb use of certain codes (escape sequences, usually embedded in text files or email messages) that remap keys on the keyboard to commands such as DELETE or FORMAT. ANSI (the American National Standards Institute) is a shorthand form that refers to the ANSI screen formatting rules. Many early MS-DOS programs relied on these rules, and required the use of the ANSI.SYS file, which also allowed keyboard remapping. The use of ANSI.SYS is very rare nowadays.

antiviral although an adjective, frequently used as a noun as a short form for *antivirus software* or systems of all types

antivirus software see *scanner, change detection, activity monitor*

antivirus virus *virus* that specifically looks for and removes other viruses. These entities cannot be said to be beneficial or useful examples of viruses, since they have generally created more problems than the viruses they remove. See *benign*.

applet small application transported over the networks, especially as an enhancement to a Web page. Applets often arrive from systems that cannot be verified as trusted. Two common applet systems are *ActiveX* and Java. Java applets are only allowed access to certain functions or information: this restriction is often referred to as the *sandbox*.

application development control process or method intended to ensure that an application continues to operate according to its specifications and continues to be available

application level gateway *firewall* system in which service is provided by processes that maintain complete TCP connection state and sequencing. Application level firewalls often re-address traffic so that outgoing traffic appears to have originated from the firewall, rather than the internal host. See also *proxy server*.

archive (1) site containing a large number of files, possibly acquired over time, and often publicly accessible. See also *ftp*, particularly anonymous ftp.

(2) file that contains a number of related files, usually in a compressed format to reduce file size and transmission (upload or download) time on electronic bulletin boards or download sites on the Internet. Most software distributed as *shareware* (or similar concepts) is distributed as an archive that contains all related programs, and documentation and possibly data files. Archived files, because of the compression, appear to be encrypted, and therefore, infected files inside archives may not be detected by virus or malware scanning software. See also *compressed executable, self-extracting*.

(3) often synonymous with *backup*

armoured virus virus that tries to prevent analysts from examining its code, particularly in terms of resistance to software forensics or *forensic programming*. The virus may use various methods to make tracing, disassembling, and reverse engineering its code more difficult.

ASCII American Standard Code for Information Interchange, a coding system that assigns numerical values to characters such as letters, numbers, punctuation, and other symbols, and used in most American manufactured computers. Often used as a synonym for *text*. ASCII allows only seven bits per character (for a total of 128 characters).

ASCII files files consisting of only ASCII characters, and generally only the printable characters. With effort, it is possible to write program files for Intel-based computers consisting only of printable characters. (An example is the *EICAR Standard Antivirus Test File*.) Windows batch (BAT) files and Visual Basic Script files are also typically plain text, but are interpreted as program files, rather than being executed as object code.

ASN.1 see *Abstract Syntax Notation One*

assembly language computer-oriented language whose instructions are symbolic and usually in one-to-one correspondence with direct computer instructions (machine language). Assembly language is generally specific to a given CPU (central processing unit), although a given CPU may have multiple assembly languages written for it. Machine language is specific to a given CPU, and there is only one machine language for a CPU.

asset entity of value to the business or enterprise, be it a computer processor, disk, network link, program, datum, or user

assurance measure of confidence that the security features and architecture of a system accurately mediate and enforce the security *policy*. The policy need not be tied solely to issues of *confidentiality*, but may address requirements for *availability*, *integrity* of data or processing, *reliability*, safety, or other factors. Assurance is often neglected in planning for security: each security function should have an assurance requirement or metric. Assurance may result from formal methods, or it may be partially determined by *audit*, *penetration testing*, *simulation*, testing, or third-party reviews.

assurance level specific level on a hierarchical scale representing successively increased confidence that a target of evaluation adequately fulfills the requirements. The Trusted Computer Security Evaluation Criteria (*TCSEC*) is one example of such a hierarchy, the *Common Criteria* is another.

assurance testing process used to determine that the security features of a system are implemented as designed, and are adequate for the proposed environment. This process may include hands-on functional testing, *penetration testing*, and/or verification.

asymmetric key encryption asymmetric *key encryption*, also known as public key encryption, uses two keys—one publicly known, and one privately held. There are key management advantages to using asymmetric encryption, although the *work factor*, and therefore the strength of the system, is felt to be weaker than for *symmetric* systems with equivalent key length.

atomic indivisible, or cannot be split up. For example, an operation may be said to do several things "atomically" if all the component functions are done immediately, and there is no chance of the operation being half-completed or of another being interspersed. Particularly used in terms of database transaction processing, where all the parts of a transaction will be done before any are "committed."

attack the act of trying to bypass security controls on a system. An attack may be *active*, resulting in the alteration of data; or *passive*, resulting in the release of data. Note: The fact that an attack is made does not necessarily mean it will succeed. The degree of success depends on the *vulnerability* of the system or activity and the effectiveness of existing *countermeasures*. Attack is often used as a synonym for a specific *exploit*. See also *brute force, denial of service, distributed denial of service, hijacking, social engineering, sniffing, spoofing, trojan horse*, and *virus*.

attack signature activities on, or alterations to, a system indicating an attack or attempted attack, and particularly a specific type of attack, often determined by examination of audit or network logs

attribute in MS-DOS and Windows systems, the characteristics representing file *permissions*

audit the collection and analysis of records of activities to assess their compliance with *security policy*

audit trail chronological record of system activities that is sufficient to enable the reconstruction, reviewing, and examination of the sequence of environments and activities surrounding or leading to an operation, a procedure, or an event in a transaction from its inception to final results. Sometimes specifically referred to as a security audit trail.

authenticate (1) to verify the identity of a user, device, or other entity in a computer system, often as a prerequisite to allowing access to resources in a system

(2) to verify the integrity of data that have been stored, transmitted, or otherwise exposed to possible unauthorized modification

authentication (1) the process of verifying identity, origin, or lack of modification of a *subject* or *object*. Authentication of a user is generally based on something the user knows, is, or has.

(2) the use of some kind of system to ensure that a file or message that purports to come from a given individual or company actually does. Many authentication systems are now looking toward public key encryption, and the calculation of a check based on the contents of the file or message, and a password or key. Related concepts are *change detection* and *integrity*.

Authentication Header (AH) Internet *IPsec* protocol (RFC 2402) designed to provide connectionless data *integrity* service and data origin *authentication* service for IP datagrams, and (optionally) to provide protection against replay attacks. AH may be used alone, in combination with the IPsec *Encapsulating Security Payload* (ESP) protocol, or in a nested fashion with tunnelling. ESP can provide the same security services as AH, and can also provide data confidentiality service. The main difference between authentication services provided by ESP and AH is the extent of the coverage; ESP does not protect IP header fields unless they are encapsulated by AH.

authentication token portable device used for authenticating a user. Authentication tokens operate by challenge/response, time-based code sequences, or other techniques. These may include paper-based lists of *one-time passwords*.

authenticator means used to confirm the identity or to verify the eligibility of a station, originator, or individual. The standard authenticators are something you have, something you are, or something you know. A common mistake is to use, as an authenticator, an entity or characteristic that is more suitable for use as an identifier. As an example, in the United States a Social Security number (SSN) is unique to an individual, and therefore suitable for identification, but the wide use and availability of this information (despite regulations to the contrary) mean that the SSN is not appropriate as authentication. (The reverse error is also made: face recognition is effective as an authenticator under the right conditions, but has spectacularly failed when used, in large-scale settings, for identification.) Sometimes referred to as authentication information.

authenticity property of being genuine and capable of being verified and trusted. It is important, in security, not to assume too much about authenticity. For example, *authentication* of identity does not prove anything about the motives, competency, or activities of the individual so identified. Checksumming of a program verifies that it has not changed, but does not prove that it was not originally intended to be malicious. See also *authenticate, authentication, validate,* and *verify.*

Authenticode Microsoft's security system for *ActiveX* controls as active Web content, and other program verification. A *digital signature* system, Authenticode verifies only that the code has not changed since it was signed, and that the certificate used to sign the code was originally issued by the *certificate authority*. Authenticode does not provide for any *sandbox* restrictions, and, at the time of writing, most systems and applications using Authenticode do not have any *certificate revocation* capabilities.

authorization the granting of *access* or other rights to a user, program, or process

AV abbreviation used to distinguish the antiviral research community (AV) from those who call themselves "virus researchers" but are primarily interested in writing and exchanging viral programs (vx). Also an abbreviation for *antivirus software*. See also *vx*.

availability the state when the system, resources, and data are in the place needed by the user, at the time the user needs them, and in the form needed by the user. Availability is one of the *three pillars* of security.

B

B1FF fictional character, possibly created by Joe Talmadge, originally used or referred to in Usenet news postings, portraying the stereotypical "newbie" (novice or newcomer) on the Net, generally a *blackhat wannabe*. Postings from B1FF typically use capital letters, deliberately misspell words, and replace letters with non-alphabetic characters (dudes=D00Dz). Because such people tend to claim "!33t" (elite) status, !33t has come to replace B1FF in more recent writings, although there are many variations in spelling for both terms. B1FF is probably the preferred one, since it looks like hexadecimal representation. No relation to the biff mail notification utility.

back door see *backdoor*

backdoor hidden software or hardware mechanism that can be triggered to permit system protection mechanisms to be circumvented. The function will generally provide unusually high, or even full, access to the system either without an account or from a normally restricted account. It is activated in some innocent-appearing manner; for example, a key sequence at a terminal. Invocation of the backdoor can also be done by sending a specific packet to a network port; see *RAT*. Software developers often introduce backdoors in their code to enable them to reenter the system and perform certain functions; see *maintenance hook*. The backdoor is sometimes left in a fully developed system either by design or by accident. Synonymous with *trap door*, which was formerly the preferred usage. Usage *back door* is also very common.

background task task executed by the system that generally remains invisible to the user. Most processes in advanced or multi-user systems operate in the background. Some *malware* is designed to be executed as a background task so the user does not realize unwanted actions are occurring. Many attacks often take advantage of loopholes in utility processes operating in the background.

backup (n) a duplicate copy of data made for archiving purposes or for protecting against damage or loss (v) the process of creating duplicate data. Some programs back up data files while maintaining both the current version and the preceding version on disk. However, a backup is not considered secure unless it is stored away from the original, and so removable media is preferred.

backup plan procedure for maintaining backups of system and user data. See *contingency plan*, *differential backup*, *full backup*, and *incremental backup*.

bacterium specialized form of *virus* that does not attach to a specific file, possibly also related to spread by electronic mail. Usage obscure: term should not be used.

BAD acronym for Broken As Designed, said of a program that is useless because of bad design rather than *bugs*

bait usually used in reference to a file, this refers to a virus *infection* target of initially known characteristics. To trap *file infectors* that insist on larger files, a string of null characters of arbitrary length is often used.

Floppy disks are, of course, used as bait for boot sector *viruses*, but the term is not often used in that way. Another name for bait files is goat or sacrificial goat files.

banner the initial message given by a system to prompt a login or identify a connection. Originally called a "welcome message," since most banners said something like "Welcome to XYZ Corp Computer System," the term *banner* is now preferred because some system intruders used the "welcome" implication to avoid prosecution.

baseline situation of a system either in normal operation, or at a particular point in time. Generally, this is measured by an image or calculation taken on a system at a given moment.

bastion host system that has been hardened to resist *attack* and is installed on a network in such a way that it is expected to come under attack. Bastion hosts are often components of *firewalls*, or may be Web servers or public access systems connected to an untrusted or public network. A *honeypot* is often a bastion host with additional *audit* and alerting functions.

battle box in *business continuity planning*, a collection of information and other resources necessary for the operation of a plan packed in a single container so as to be readily available and transportable as needed. See also *go bag*.

behaviour monitor see *activity monitor*

behaviour blocker see *operation restrictor*

Bell-La Padula model formal state transition model of computer security policy that describes a set of access control rules. In this formal model, the entities in a computer system are divided into abstract sets of *subjects* and *objects*. The notion of a secure state is defined, and it is proven that each state transition preserves security by moving from secure state to secure state, thereby inductively proving that the system is secure. A system state is defined to be "secure" if the only permitted access modes of subjects to objects are in accordance with a specific security *policy*. In order to determine whether a specific access mode is allowed, the clearance of a subject is compared to the *classification* of the object, and a determination is made as to whether the subject is authorized for the specific access mode.

More specifically, Bell-La Padula is concerned with *confidentiality*. Subjects in the model are forbidden from obtaining (reading) information from an object of higher classification, and from divulging (writing) information to an object of lower classification. See star property (*-*property*) and *simple security property*.

benign somewhat careless term often used to describe a *virus* that appears not to be intentionally malicious in that it does not carry an obviously damaging *payload* code section. Since viral programs may cause problems simply by the use of system resources or the modification of files, many are of the opinion that a benign or good virus is impossible.

benign environment non-hostile environment that may be protected from external hostile elements by physical, personnel, and procedural security counter-measures

best practice the *gold standard* for security buzzphrases. In fact, there was an extended discussion on the use of the phrase "best practice" on the CISSPforum in July 2005. The implication of best practice is that it is an optimum procedure for most situations, although it may also imply a practice that works in every situation, or a minimum standard. It was, how-ever, noted that "best practice" is never a guarantee or panacea. Other phrases discussed were standard practice (what most people do), essential practice (what should be done as an absolute minimum), and leading practice (what the "best" companies do).

between-the-lines entry unauthorized access obtained by tapping the temporarily inactive terminal of a legiti-mate user. See *hijacking*, and *piggyback*. The general condition is referred to as TOC/TOU (Time Of Check versus Time Of Use, pronounced like "talk to"), meaning a discrepancy between the time of a check being made, and the time the resource is used.

beyond A1 level of trust defined by the Department of Defense Trusted Computer System Evaluation Criteria (*TCSEC*) that is beyond the technology available at the time the criteria were developed. It includes all the A1-level features plus additional ones not required at the A1 level.

bimodal virus see *multipartite*

biometric pertaining to the measurement of the human body: in security terms, relating to means of *authentication* based on patterns unique to an individual's body, such as fingerprints and retinal patterns, or behaviour, such as voiceprints or handwriting

BIOS Basic Input/Output System, the "hardwired" firmware programming used to start the *boot* process in *ISA*/Wintel computers. The BIOS is located in the *ROM* area of the system and is usually stored permanently. There are many BIOS versions in ISA/Wintel computers, but they generally assume the operating system will be interrupt driven (as MS-DOS is), and start to set up structures to support that model. Since *boot sector infectors* run before the operating system starts, and require only the BIOS programming, they are sometimes called BIOS viruses, although the term can create confusion and should be avoided. Some computers now use EEPROM (Electrically Erasable Programmable Read Only Memory), and at least one virus now tries to erase such "flash" BIOS programming. Otherwise, BIOS cannot be infected or corrupted by a virus.

bit error rate the number of erroneous bits divided by the total number of bits transmitted, received, or processed over some period of time. Also bit error ratio. Abbreviated BER.

blackhat communities or individuals who attempt to break into computer systems without prior authorization, or explore security primarily from an *attack* perspective. The term originates from old American western genre movies where the "good guys" always wore white hats and the "bad guys" always wore black. See also *whitehat*.

block cipher *crypto-algorithm* that *encrypts* data in discrete blocks of a given size, rather than as a continuous stream of bits. Compare with *stream cipher*.

boot to start (cold boot) or reset (warm boot) the computer. The term arises from the phrase "bootstrap program," and the idea of lifting oneself by one's own bootstraps, or starting with no support.

boot record the program recorded in the first physical or logical sector mounted on the disk drive, and containing software to get the computer to a working state. The term is most commonly used in connection with *ISA* or Wintel computers, where there are actually two boot records: the *master boot record* (dealing with disk and hardware structure), and the *system boot record* (containing pointers to operating system files). See also *boot sector*.

boot sector generically, the first sector, or sectors, on any disk, usually containing programming necessary for the *boot* process. In *ISA* or Wintel computers, the term is not well defined, although it is generally accepted to be the *system boot record*, and thus the first physical sector on floppy diskettes and the first logical sector on hard disks. For precision in dealing with security issues and concerns, it is best to refer specifically to the *master boot record* or system boot record.

boot sector infector (BSI) *virus* that places its starting code in the boot sector, thus being run before any programming, including the operating system. A BSI is able to take control of interrupts and machine functions, may be able to subvert some protection and detection measures, and is also considered a virus of the base computer hardware, rather than of the operating system. In *ISA* computers, when MS-DOS was the dominant operating system and before widespread use of public networks for data transfer, BSIs were the most successful form of virus, and were considered *BIOS* viruses. Some BIOS boot sector infectors occupied the *master boot record*, while others inhabited the *system boot record*: in most cases, the displaced record was moved to an unused sector of the disk so control could be passed to it once the virus had run, and thus the computer would appear to have a normal *boot* process. Also known as boot sector virus, BSV.

boot sector virus see *boot sector infector*

bounce message notification message returned to the sender by a site unable to relay email to the intended recipient. Reasons might include a nonexistent or misspelled username, or a relay site that is down.

bounds checking testing of computer program results for access to storage outside authorized or proper limits

Brain almost certainly the first *virus* written in the MS-DOS computing environment that became widespread among normal computer users. An example of a "strict" *boot sector infector* and the earliest known use of *stealth* virus programming. Sometimes referred to as "Brain (C)" or "(C) Brain" due to the presence of the string "(C) 1986 Brain" in the body of the virus. (Many books and articles use the copyright symbol instead of the "(C)" string, but the copyright symbol does not appear in the body of the virus.)

breach the successful and repeatable defeat of security controls with or without an arrest of the system itself, which could result in penetration of the system

break to stop a program temporarily, so it may be debugged. The place where it stops is a "breakpoint."

British Standard 7799 (BS7799) standard code of practice and guidance on how to secure an information system, and the management framework, objectives, and control requirements for information security management systems, in three, increasingly detailed, parts. Versions were subsequently accepted as ISO Standards 17799, 27001, and 27002.

Brooks' Law "Adding manpower to a late software project makes it later," a result of the fact that the advantage from splitting work among N programmers is expected to be proportional to N, but the overhead costs associated with coordinating their work is proportional to the square of N. The quote is from Fred Brooks, a manager of IBM's OS/360 project and author of *The Mythical Man-Month*, an excellent early book on software engineering.

browsing the act of searching through storage to locate or acquire information without necessarily knowing the existence or the format of the information being sought

brute force *attack* methodology whereby all possible options are used in turn, usually in a programmed sequence attempting to use all possible *passwords* or *decryption keys*. See also *dictionary attack*.

BS7799 see *British Standard 7799*

BSI see *boot sector infector*

BSV see *boot sector infector*

buffer overflow common program error in which input is not checked for length. Excessive input may overflow the memory allotted and, if not discarded, may create a situation where the program can be forced to execute arbitrary code or switch operation control to an arbitrary location.

bug unintentional fault, generally in programming code or implementation, that may make a system fail or behave in unexpected ways, and, in any case, causes actions that neither the programmer nor the user planned. Common examples of bugs are *buffer overflows*, *loopholes*, or *maintenance hooks* left in place when a project is complete. An error of design is more correctly referred to as a *flaw*.
Computer mythology credits Grace Murray Hopper with the invention of the term "bug," but it was known to have been used in engineering circles in the nineteenth century, and Hopper herself referred to the "[f]irst actual case of bug being found" in a

machine. The "moth in the Mark II," and its subsequent use as an excuse to Howard Aiken when he asked why the machine was not "makin' numbers," may have been the origin of the use of "debugging" as a verb. The bug can be seen online courtesy of the Smithsonian institution at http://americanhistory.si.edu/csr/comphist/objects/bug.htm.

build often the final compilation of a software system, but also the particular program that results. Thus, a build is similar to a version of software, except that build is generally more precise. Security and *vulnerability* assessments of software will be based on a given build, and applying an assessment to other versions could result in incorrect conclusions. See also *system model*.

business continuity plan (BCP) plan and preparations directed toward the immediate recovery of systems critical to the function of the business, or to the ability of the business to operate in the temporary absence of important systems. Activities related to the preparation and maintenance of such a plan are usually referred to as business continuity management. See also *contingency plan* and *disaster recovery plan*.

business impact analysis (BIA) assessment of the effects and potential loss resulting from an *incident* that might affect *business continuity*. Similar, but not identical, to *risk analysis*.

C

call back procedure for identifying a remote terminal. In a call back, the host system disconnects the caller and then dials the authorized telephone number of the remote terminal to reestablish the connection. Of limited use for remote access, and recently subject to failure because of call forwarding technologies. Synonymous with dial back or ring back.

call tree structured and generally cascading process for contacting personnel in an emergency, particularly in *business continuity planning*. See also *fan out*.

capability protected identifier that identifies the *object* and specifies the *access rights* to be allowed to the accessor (or *subject*) who possesses the capability. In a capability-based system, access to protected objects such as files is granted if the would-be subject possesses a capability for the object. This can also be used for *authentication* (by seeing the system as an object). Due to the protection of the capability identifier, the ability to assume false authorization is reduced. Often implemented as capability tables.

category restrictive label that has been applied to *classified* or *unclassified* data as a means of increasing the protection of the data and further restricting access to the data

cavity virus type of *overwriting virus* that overwrites either slack space within or behind the target program file, or sections of null data within the file, such that it can infect the host file without increasing the length

of the file while also preserving the host's functionality. Usage rare.

CERT the Computer Emergency Response Team established at the Software Engineering Institute (SEI) of
Carnegie-Mellon University after the 1988 Internet
worm attack. Recently, the preferred reference has
been CERT/CC (Computer Emergency Response
Team Coordination Center). CMU has apparently
obtained exclusive use of the name CERT, and recommends that other emergency teams style themselves as CIRTs (Computer Incident Response
Teams).

certificate *digitally signed* statement that contains information about an entity and the entity's *public key*

certificate revocation list (CRL) document maintained
and published by a *certification authority* listing those
certificates previously issued by the CA that are no
longer valid

certification the comprehensive evaluation of the technical and nontechnical security features of a system
and other *safeguards*, made in support of the *accreditation* process, that establishes the extent to which a
particular design and implementation meets a specified set of security requirements. Note that certification has no relation to an asymmetric key
encryption *certificate*, or the related authorities
and lists.

certification authority (CA) central authority for key
management in an overall system for the use of
asymmetric encryption known as a public key

infrastructure, or *PKI*. Certification authority, for some reason, is generally capitalized, and is usually referred to by the acronym CA. CA may refer to an individual office or server, but a single CA is usually part of a hierarchy, and certification authority may refer to the entire hierarchy as well.

chain letter message directing the recipient to send out multiple copies so its circulation increases in a geometric progression as long as the instructions are carried out. The chain letter is usually described as having a tripartite structure: a hook to catch interest, a threat to persuade the recipient to comply, and a request to copy and spread the message. The content of the chain letter message often mentions spreading luck, friendship, some type of urban legend, or a warning of some kind. A chain letter is a type of *spam*, and a *virus alert hoax* is a type of chain letter.

Challenge Handshake Authentication Protocol (CHAP) peer entity *authentication* method for PPP (Point to Point Protocol), using a randomly generated challenge and requiring a matching response that depends on a *cryptographic* hash of the challenge and a secret *key*

challenge/response security procedure in which one communicator requests *authentication* of another communicator, and the latter replies with a response based on data provided by the first. The concepts of challenge/response, *initialization vector, nonce, salt*, and see*d* are closely related. Challenge/response is generally used in regard to password and authentication schemes, initialization vector to block ciphers, nonce to short, automated network messages, salt to password storage, and seed to *pseudorandom* number generation.

change control management tool to provide control and traceability for all changes made to the system. Often, reference is made to change management.

change detection *antiviral* software that looks for changes in the computer system. A *virus* must change something, and it is assumed that program files, disk system areas, and certain areas of memory should not change. This software is often referred to as integrity checking software, but it does not necessarily protect the integrity of data, nor does it always assess the reasons for a possibly valid change. Change detection using strong encryption is sometimes also known as *authentication* software.

change management formal process for requesting, specifying, approving, developing (or acquiring), testing, and accepting changes to a software system. Generally, change management involves new programming, or a new purchase of software. Depending on the criticality of the system, similarly formal processes may be applied to *configuration* changes, or the application of patches (which may involve protection against security *vulnerabilities*). (Note that managers in non-technical environments may define change management as any process to reduce disruption from any change to operations.)

CHAP see *Challenge Handshake Authentication Protocol*

checkpoint known situation or state of the system or process, from which processing may continue or be restarted in the case of a failure or other problem

checksum calculation based on the content of data, which, if performed at one time and then compared against the same calculation at a later time, can be used to determine if the content of the data has changed. In its strictest form, a checksum is a calculation based on adding or summing up all the bytes or 1-bits in a file or message. *Parity* bits in asynchronous transmission are a type of checksum. The term is sometimes carelessly used to refer to all methods of *change detection* or *authentication* that rely on some level of calculation based on file contents, such as *cyclic redundancy checking* (CRC).

chosen-ciphertext attack *cryptanalysis* technique in which the analyst tries to determine the *key* from knowledge of *plaintext* that corresponds to *ciphertext* selected or dictated by the analyst

chosen-plaintext attack *cryptanalysis* technique in which the analyst tries to determine the *key* from knowledge of *ciphertext* that corresponds to *plaintext* selected or dictated by the analyst

CHRISTMA exec specific example of a viral type of email message, the earliest known script email *virus*, using the REXX scripting language. This message was released in December 1987. The user was asked to type "CHRISTMA" to generate an electronic Christmas card, but was not told that the program also made, and mailed, copies of itself during the display. (Within the virus research community, the form "CHRISTMA EXEC" is used almost universally. The more correct form is "CHRISTMA exec," since REXX scripts were referred to as "execs" to distinguish them from the earlier EXEC language in IBM mainframes.)

CIAC see *Computer Incident Advisory Capability*

cipher *cryptographic algorithm* for *encryption* and *decryption*

cipher block chaining (CBC) *block cipher* mode that enhances *electronic codebook* mode by chaining together blocks of *ciphertext* it produces. This mode operates by combining (*exclusive OR-ing*) the algorithm's ciphertext output block with the next *plaintext* block to form the next input block for the algorithm.

cipher feedback (CFB) *block cipher* mode that enhances *electronic codebook* mode by chaining together the blocks of *ciphertext* it produces and operating on *plaintext* segments of variable length less than or equal to the block length. This mode operates by using the previously generated ciphertext segment as the algorithm's input (i.e., by "feeding back" the ciphertext) to generate an output block, and then combining (*exclusive OR-ing*) that output block with the next plaintext segment (block length or less) to form the next ciphertext segment.

ciphertext apparently random string of data, conveying little or no information to an unauthorized entity, but from which an original message or *plaintext* can be extracted by means of an appropriate *key* and algorithm

ciphertext-only attack *cryptanalysis* technique in which the analyst tries to determine the *key* solely from knowledge of intercepted *ciphertext* (although the analyst may also know other clues, such as the *cryptographic algorithm*, the language in which the *plaintext* was written, the subject matter of the plaintext, and some probable plaintext words)

classification (1) a grouping of classified information to which a hierarchical, restrictive security label is applied to increase protection of the data (2) the level of protection required to be applied to that information. See also *security level*.

classified refers to information that is formally required by a security policy to be given data confidentiality service and to be marked with a security label to indicate its protected status. The term is mainly used in government, especially in the military, and particularly in the United States Department of Defense. See also *unclassified*.

cleartext *unencrypted* data, also known as *plaintext*

client system entity that requests and uses a service or resource provided by another system entity (the server)

client-server model of network operation where services and resources are requested by the *client* and fulfilled by the server. The significance to security is that security policy should be (but is not always) enforced by the server. In peer-to-peer models of networking, a more complex security model must generally be implemented.

closed security environment environment in which both of the following conditions hold true:
(1) application developers (including maintainers) have sufficient clearances and authorizations to provide an acceptable presumption that they have not introduced malicious logic.
(2) *configuration control* provides sufficient *assurance* that applications and the equipment are protected against the introduction of malicious logic prior to and during the operation of system applications.

cluster virus *virus* that makes a change to disk or directory structure data such that when a valid program is invoked, the virus is run first. Because the data to be changed is very small, it can be altered very rapidly, affecting large numbers of files in a short space of time, and therefore these viruses were sometimes called fast infectors. Also known as FAT virus (after the MS-DOS *File Allocation Table* directory structure), sector virus, and *system virus*.

CMOS stands for complementary metal oxide semiconductor. This technology is used in a form of memory that can be held in the computer, while the main power is off, with low-power battery backup. CMOS memory is used in MS-DOS/*BIOS*/*ISA* computers to hold small tables of information regarding the basic hardware of the system. Since the memory is maintained while the power is off, there is a myth that *viruses* can hide in the CMOS. (CMOS memory is too small, and the contents are never executed as a program.) Also, when the battery power fails, the computer is temporarily unusable. This is often attributed, falsely, to viral activity.

CObIT Control Objectives for Information and related Technology, the set of IT control objectives published by the Information Systems Audit and Control Association (ISACA), the body that certifies IT security auditors

code (1) in computer terminology, refers to either human (source) or machine (object) readable programming or fragments thereof. Since *viruses*, before they attach to a host program, are not complete programs, they are often referred to as code to distinguish them from programs that are complete in themselves. (2) a system of symbols used to represent information, which might originally have had some other meaning. This is often seen as synonymous with *cipher* or *encryption*, but codes usually have fixed meaning relations, rather than algorithmic transformations of data. In some cases, specialized types of codes may be applied to or embedded with data, supplying redundant information for purposes such as error detection and correction. See *forward error correction* and *Hamming code*.

Code Red the first variant of a family that possibly included the almost equally well-known *Nimda*. Code Red infected Internet servers running the Microsoft IIS (Internet Information Server) software, and used a known bug in that program to infect new machines. Probably due to the popularity of the IIS server on low maintenance sites, Code Red infected approximately 350,000 machines within 9 to 13 hours. Despite this success, Code Red was never as dangerous as it was made out to be, and was definitely a *media virus*.

cold site in *business continuity planning* or *disaster recovery planning*, an *alternate site* with necessary electrical and service connections, but no running system, maintained by an organization to facilitate prompt resumption of service after a disaster. Some organizations now refer to "gradual recovery." See also *warm site, hot site*.

command centre central point for coordination of activities for emergency operations or *business continuity*

commercial programs that are sold either directly from the manufacturer or through normal retail channels, as opposed to shareware. Users are often told to "buy only commercial" as a defence against *virus infections* or other types of *malware*. In fact, there is very little risk of obtaining viruses from shareware, and there are many known instances of viral programs infecting commercial software. In terms of other forms of malware, it is often proposed that the number of serious bugs in any new commercial software may rival the number of *trojan* programs released in any given period of time. See also *freeware, public domain, open source,* and *shareware*.

Common Criteria an attempt to harmonize the various national security standards and security philosophies. See *Common Criteria for Information Technology Security*.

Common Criteria for Information Technology Security the Common Criteria is a standard for evaluating information technology products and systems, such as operating systems, computer networks, distributed systems, and applications. It states requirements for security functions and for assurance measures. Canada, France, Germany, the Netherlands, the United Kingdom, and the United States (NIST and NSA) began developing this standard in 1993, based on the European ITSEC, the Canadian Trusted Computer Product Evaluation Criteria (CTCPEC), and the United States "Federal Criteria for Information Technology Security" (FC) and its precursor, the *TCSEC*. Version 2.1 of the Criteria is equivalent to ISO's International Standard 15408 (I15408).

communications security (COMSEC) measures taken to deny unauthorized persons information derived from telecommunications of the United States Government concerning national security, and to ensure the authenticity of such telecommunications. Communications security includes cryptosecurity, transmission security, emission security, and physical security of communications security material and information.

companion virus type of *virus* that does not actually attach to another program, but interposes itself into the chain of command, so that the virus is executed before the infected program. Most often, this is done by using a similar name and the rules of program precedence to associate itself with a regular program. Also referred to as a spawning virus.

compartment class of information that has need-to-know access controls beyond those normally provided for access to multilevel security. Related to *multilateral security* and the *lattice model.*

compartmented security mode see *modes of operation*

compensation control see *controls*

compressed executable program file that has been compressed to save disk space, and automatically returns to executable form when invoked. Because compression appears to be a form of encryption, programs that are infected with a *virus* before being compressed, or those that contain other forms of *malware*, may hide the infection from *scanning* software. See also *archive*, and *self-extracting.*

compromise (v) to perform an action not in accordance with the *security policy*, or to cause a system to do so (n) a violation of the security policy of a system such that unauthorized disclosure of sensitive information may have occurred

compromising emanations unintentional data-related or intelligence-bearing signals that, if intercepted and analyzed, disclose the information transmission received, handled, or otherwise processed by any information processing equipment. See *TEMPEST.*

computer abuse the misuse, alteration, disruption, or destruction of data processing resources. The key aspect is that it is intentional and improper.

computer cryptography the use of a *crypto-algorithm* in a computer, microprocessor, or microcomputer to perform *encryption* or *decryption* to protect information or to authenticate users, sources, or information. U.S. government or military term.

computer forensics originally the full means of obtaining legal evidence from computers and computer use, computer forensics is now limited to recovery of data from computers and computer media. Computer forensics has therefore become only one part of *digital forensics*.

computer fraud computer-related crimes involving deliberate misrepresentation, alteration, or disclosure of data to obtain something of value (usually for monetary gain). A computer system must have been involved in the perpetration or cover-up of the act or series of acts. A computer system might have been involved through improper manipulation of input data; output or results; applications programs; data files; computer operations; communications; or computer hardware, systems software, or firmware.

Computer Incident Advisory Capability (CIAC) computer emergency response team within the U.S. Department of Energy, this group is widely known for a series of highly regarded messages and postings about security vulnerabilities

computer security audit independent evaluation of the controls employed to ensure appropriate protection of an organization's information *assets*. A formal security audit has goals and procedures somewhat different from the normal and ongoing *audit* process.

computer security subsystem device designed to provide limited computer security features in a larger system environment

Computer Security Technical Vulnerability Reporting Program (CSTVRP) program that focuses on technical vulnerabilities in commercially available hardware, firmware, and software products acquired by the U.S. Department of Defense. CSTVRP provides for the reporting, catalouging, and discrete dissemination of technical vulnerability and corrective measure information to Department of Defense components on a need-to-know basis.

computer viral program Rob Slade's own invention. In an attempt to avoid the fights over what constitutes a "true" virus, he uses the term "viral" to refer to self-reproducing programs regardless of other distinctions. So far, he's gotten away with it.

concealment system method of achieving confidentiality in which sensitive information is hidden by embedding it in irrelevant data. See also *steganography*.

Concept probably the first Microsoft Word macro *virus*, and certainly the first macro virus to be successful *in the wild*

confidentiality the concept of holding sensitive data in confidence, limited to an appropriate set of individuals or organizations. Confidentiality is considered one of the *three pillars* of security.

configuration control the process of controlling modifications to the system's hardware, firmware, software, and documentation that provides sufficient *assurance* that the system is protected against the introduction of improper modifications prior to, during, and after system implementation. Compare *configuration management*.

configuration management the management of security related features and assurances through control of changes made to a system's configuration. Historically, this involved any changes to a system (see *configuration control*), but more recently it has been seen to involve configuration that is short of changes to the software (see *change management*).

confinement the prevention of the leaking of sensitive data from a program

confinement channel synonymous with *covert channel*. Archaic usage.

confinement property see star property (*-property*)

contamination (1) the intermixing of data at different sensitivity and need-to-know levels. The lower level data is said to be contaminated by the higher level data; thus, the contaminating (higher level) data may not receive the required level of protection. (2) similarly for data of varying *integrity* or corruption

contingency plan plan for emergency response, backup operations, and post-disaster recovery that will ensure the availability of critical resources and facilitate the continuity of operations in an emergency situation. May be synonymous with disaster plan and emergency plan, but most commonly held to be specifically related to information systems. See also *disaster recovery plan* and *business continuity plan*.

control zone the space, expressed in feet of radius, surrounding equipment processing sensitive information, that is under sufficient (primarily) physical and (possibly) technical control to preclude an unauthorized entry or compromise

controlled access see *access control*

controlled sharing the condition that exists when *access control* is applied to all users and components of a system

controls an important, but strangely ill-defined, area of security, very similar to *safeguards* and *countermeasures*, used to prevent failures of *integrity*, *availability*, and *confidentiality*. Controls are grouped and discussed in a number of not quite orthogonal ways. One way of dividing controls (sometimes referring to categories) examines administrative (policies, procedures, etc.), physical (locks, guards, etc.), and technical (encryption, network auditing, etc.) controls. Another way of classifying (sometimes referring to types) surveys preventative/preventive (deterring and blocking an event), detective (determining and investigating an event), corrective (restoring and recovering from an event), deterrent (increasing perceived risk to an attacker), recovery (restoring lost resources), and compensation (provision of redundancy or other means to counteract loss of resources) controls. *Access control* is considered a special case, but may also be considered preventative/preventive and technical controls. However, access controls could also be considered administrative and deterrent controls. As you can see, these divisions are not always clear.

cookie (1) a small piece of data originally intended to maintain state between Web browser accesses to a site. (HTTP [HyperText Transfer Protocol] 1.0 did not provide for persistent connections.) Because the data is stored on the user's computer, and because it is possible to store the data in such a way as to allow it to be world readable, careless setting of cookies, or the ubiquitous presence of an entity on many Web sites, may create a situation in which a user's *privacy* is at risk.

(2) the term has been used to indicate some form of *authentication* information or ticket, and is specifically used for a piece of data in the *ISAKMP* security association negotiation, but these usages are relatively rare

copyleft the rights notice (General Public License) carried by GNU EMACS and other Free Software Foundation software, granting modification, reuse, and reproduction rights to all users. The term is used in somewhat ironic contradistinction to *copyright*, where the creator is granted control, and the right to restrict usage of, the creation. See also *General Public Virus.*

copyright the right of the author of a written or artistic work to control the use and distribution of the work. One of the basic *intellectual property* rights, the others of which are patent, trademark, and trade secret.

core wars computer game in which two or more programs attempt to destroy each other inside a real or simulated computer. Originally played with real programs in the earliest timesharing computers and inspired by the operations of rogue programs in early multi-tasking machines. Because one of the successful strategies was to create a program that submitted copies of itself to various places in the address space, this game is often seen as a precursor of *viruses* and *worms*, and is often discussed in connection with the battle between malicious software and protective software developers. Core Wars (capitalized) is now a standardized game using a simulated machine language called Redstone code (or redcode).

The earliest formal example of core wars was DARWIN, conceived and developed in 1961 by V. A. Vyssotsky, M. Douglas McIlroy, and Bob Morris at Bell Telephone Laboratories in Murray Hill, New Jersey. It ran on an IBM 7090 mainframe under the Bell Labs operating system.

corrective control see *controls*

cost–benefit analysis the assessment of the costs of providing data protection for a system versus the cost of losing or compromising the data. Sometimes also known as cost-risk analysis.

countermeasure any action, device, procedure, technique, or other measure that reduces the vulnerability of or threat to a system. See also *safeguard*.

covert channel communications channel that allows two cooperating processes to transfer information in a manner that violates the system's security *policy*. More specifically, a means of information leaking from a system via a channel not normally considered a communications medium. Synonymous with *confinement channel*.

covert storage channel *covert channel* that involves the direct or indirect writing of a storage location by one process, and the direct or indirect reading of the storage location by another process. Covert storage channels typically involve a resource (such as sectors on a disk) that is shared by two *subjects* at different security levels.

covert timing channel *covert channel* in which one process signals information to another by modulating its own use of system resources (for example, CPU time) in such a way that this manipulation affects the real response time observed by the second process

crab originally, "crabs" was a prank program on Macintosh and Atari computers that erased the screen display by having graphical crabs "eat" it. An obscure usage refers to malicious software that erases screen displays. (There are very few examples of this type of activity.)

cracker (1) someone who tries to break the security of, and gain access to, someone else's system without being invited to do so. This is, of course, an attempt to avoid the controversial usage of the term *hacker*. A more specific usage is that referring to software piracy aficionados (*warez* d00dz) who actually perform the cracking of copy protection codes, rather than simply distributing the pirated packages. See *also adversary*, *intruder*, and *blackhat*. (2) person who drives a pickup truck and objects to definition (1)

CRC see *cyclic redundancy check*

critical (1) a condition of a service or other system resource such that denial of access to, or lack of availability of, that resource would jeopardize a system user's ability to perform a primary function or would result in other serious consequences (2) each extension of an X.509 certificate (or CRL) is marked as being either critical or non-critical. If an extension is critical and a certificate user (or CRL user) does not recognize the extension type or does not implement its semantics, the user is required to treat the certificate (or CRL) as invalid.

CRL see *certificate revocation list*

crossover error rate (CER) if the *false acceptance rate* and *false rejection rate* are graphed as the sensitivity of a security system is varied, *false acceptance* will start at a high value and fall, whereas *false rejection* will start with a low value and climb. The point at which the graph of the FAR crosses that of the FRR is the crossover error rate, and is generally considered a reasonable overall measure of the accuracy of a system. (It is easy to demonstrate situations in which the CER is not the best measure or setting for a system.)

cryptanalysis the science that deals with analysis of a *cryptographic* system to gain knowledge needed to break or circumvent the protection the system is designed to provide. In some cases, this would be conversion of *ciphertext* to *plaintext*, but in other cases, it might involve forging of *digital signatures* or *certificates*. The basic cryptanalytic attacks on *encryption* systems are *ciphertext-only*, *known-plaintext*, *chosen-plaintext*, and *chosen-ciphertext*; and these generalize to the other kinds of cryptography. See also *cryptology*.

crypto formerly widely used as an abbreviation for *cryptography*, *cryptographic*, *cryptology*, or even *encryption*, this term probably should not be used because of the potential for misunderstanding

cryptographic algorithm well-defined procedure or sequence of rules or steps used to produce a key stream or *ciphertext* from *plaintext*, and vice versa. Older usage is crypto-algorithm.

cryptographic checksum one-way function applied to a file to produce a unique "fingerprint" of the file for later reference. Often part of the process of creating a *digital signature*.

cryptographic key see *key*

cryptography the principles, means, and methods for rendering information unintelligible, and for restoring encrypted information to intelligible form. Literally, hidden writing.

cryptology slightly more general field than *cryptography*, cryptology includes *cryptanalysis*, or code breaking, and code making

cryptoperiod the time span during which a particular *key* is authorized to be used in a *cryptographic* system, an aspect of key management. Also known as key life-time and validity period.

cryptosecurity the security or protection resulting from the proper use of technically sound *cryptosystems*

cryptosystem complete and functional system for *cryptography*, including a sound *crypto-algorithm*, provisions for the required functions of the system, and proper key choice and management

cryptovariable becoming the preferred form of *key*

cyclic redundancy check (CRC) version of *change detection* that performs calculation on the data in a file or message as a matrix. This can detect multiple or subtle changes that ordinary *checksum* calculations miss. Also used extensively in data communications for ensuring the integrity of file transfers.

cypherpunk community of users and developers dedicated to creating systems for anonymous communications and network access. Since the cypherpunk community is generally opposed to any invasion of privacy or any form of surveillance, the law enforcement community generally perceives them in a negative light. Unfortunately, there does seem to be a relation between certain segments of the cypherpunk community and some groups engaged in software piracy and other forms of intellectual property theft.

D

DAC see *Discretionary Access Control*

DAME Dark Avenger's Mutation Engine. See *MtE*.

Dark Avenger the pseudonym of a Bulgarian virus writer thought to be responsible for the "Eddie" family of viral programs (among others) and the *polymorphic* code known as the *MtE*

dark side hacker criminal or malicious *hacker, cracker,* or *blackhat.* The reference is from the *Star Wars* saga: the dark side of the Force is evil. The opposite of a dark-side hacker is a samurai, a specifically technical type of *whitehat.*

data diddling generally refers to an activity that makes small, random, or incremental changes to information, rather than complete erasure of files or purposeful changing of data. Use of this term is not recommended since the phrase is vague and there is little agreement on meaning.

Data Encryption Algorithm (DEA) *symmetric block cipher,* defined as part of the U.S. government's *Data Encryption Standard.* Generally speaking, in U.S. government systems, there will be an algorithm, which is the mathematical engine, and a standard, which is the fully working implementation.

Data Encryption Standard (DES) cryptographic algorithm for the protection of unclassified data, published in United States Federal Information Processing Standard (FIPS) 46. The DES, which was approved by the National Institute of Standards and Technology, was intended for public and government use. A stronger version is provided by *triple DES* (or 3DES), which comes in a variety of forms. The grand old DES algorithm is no longer the officially sanctioned standard.

data flow control synonymous with *information flow control*

data integrity the property that data are unmodified, or meet an expectation of quality

data mirror system whereby data writes or other disk activity is written to two or more disks simultaneously so if one fails, the data is still available

data owner the authority, individual, or organization that has original responsibility for the data by statute, executive order, or directive

data security the protection of data from unauthorized (accidental or intentional) modification, destruction, or disclosure

DDoS Distributed Denial of Service. A form of network *denial of service* (DoS) *attack* in which a master computer controls a number of client computers to flood the target (or victim) with traffic, using *backdoor* agent, client, or *zombie* software on a number of client machines. The master computer will attempt to control these machines and coordinate an attack on a target. The master computer never contacts the target directly, and the large number of zombie machines multiplies the force of the attack. The zombie program is generally distributed as some form of *trojan horse*, although zombies may be installed if control has already been obtained by means of a remote access trojan (*RAT*). Usage of the acronym DDoS in preference to the full phrase is almost universal.

DEA see *Data Encryption Algorithm*

DEADBEEF the hexadecimal word-fill pattern for freshly allocated memory (decimal -21524111) under a number of IBM environments, including the RS/6000. Some modern debugging tools deliberately fill freed memory with this value.

deadlock situation wherein two or more processes are unable to proceed because each is waiting for one of the others to do something. An example arises in database management, where two users may have obtained permission to update a given record, but are unable to do so because the record is locked awaiting the update. Another is a program communicating to a server, which may find itself waiting for output from the server before sending anything more to it, while the server is similarly waiting for more input from the controlling program before outputting anything.

deception to present false or forged *identity* or *authentication* to break *security policy*. See *also social engineering*, and *spoofing*.

decipher see *decryption*

declassification administrative decision or procedure to remove or reduce the security classification of the *object* or information

decryption the process of extracting an original message, or *plaintext*, from a *ciphertext* by the application of an appropriate *key* and algorithm

dedicated security mode see *modes of operation*

default account system login account that has been pre-defined in a manufactured system to permit access when the system is first put into service. Sometimes, the default username and password are the same in each copy of the system. In any case, when the system is put into service, the *default password* should immediately be changed or the default account should be disabled.

default classification temporary classification reflecting the highest classification being processed in a system. The default classification is included in the caution statement affixed to the *object*.

default password the password on system administration or service accounts when a system is shipped from the manufacturer. Failing to change default passwords or *default accounts* is a major security risk.

defence in depth security approach whereby each system on the network is secured to the greatest possible degree, using layers of defences whereby penetrations successful at one point will be caught by another *safeguard*

degauss to reduce magnetic flux density to zero by applying a reverse magnetizing field. Degaussing destroys information on magnetic media: hence the warning not to store backup floppies by sticking them to your computer with a magnet.

degausser electrical device that can generate a magnetic field for the purpose of degaussing magnetic storage media

degree of trust level of confidence in security mechanisms and procedures to correctly enforce a specified *security policy*

delayed disclosure form of *vulnerability disclosure* in which information about the vulnerability is not released to the general public until it has first been made known to the product vendor

DES see *Data Encryption Standard*

denial of service (DoS) any action or series of actions that prevent any part of a system from functioning in accordance with its intended purpose. This includes any action that causes unauthorized delay of service. More specifically, DoS refers to an action that does not destroy data or resources, but prevents access or use. In network operations, flooding a node or link with traffic is an effective form of denial of service. This form of malicious *attack* is particularly suited to *viruses* where no data is actually erased or corrupted, but where system resources are occupied to the extent that normal service is restricted. The *CHRISTMA exec* did not corrupt data, but occupied mail links to the point where normal transfers could not take place. The *Internet Worm* did not erase files, but multiple copies of the process eventually meant almost all processing was devoted to the Worm. Modern Internet DoS attacks typically try to flood a machine with synchronization requests from non-existent addresses. Not to be confused with DOS, which stands for Disk Operating System, and particularly the MS-DOS operating system and its variants. Synonymous with interdiction. Usage of the phrase (denial of service) or the acronym (DoS) is inconsistent, although there is a slight preference for the full phrase to avoid confusion with DOS.

dependency reliance of one process, component, or resource upon the existence or operation of another. Failure to analyze dependencies may result in lack of provision for *single points of failure*.

Descriptive Top-Level Specification (DTLS) top-level specification that is written in a natural language (e.g., English), an informal design notation, or a combination of the two

Designated Approving Authority (DAA) the official who has the authority to decide on accepting the security safeguards prescribed for an Automated Information System (*AIS*), or that official who may be responsible for issuing an *accreditation* statement that records the decision to accept those *safeguards*. U.S. government or military.

detective control see *controls*

deterrent control see *controls*

dial back synonymous with *call back*

dial-up the service whereby a computer terminal can use the telephone to initiate and effect communication with a computer or network

dictionary attack version of a *brute force* attack, refined by the assumption that, for example, passwords are more likely to be real words rather than random character strings, and so trying only words found in a dictionary file, or other common source

differential backup *backup* process that copies only such items that have been changed since the last *full backup*. A differential backup plan requires only the last full backup and the latest differential backup for complete restoration. See also *incremental backup*.

Diffie-Hellman algorithm (DH) public key (*asymmetric*) algorithm primarily used for secure key exchange. In 1976, Whitfield Diffie and Martin Hellman published the first paper to describe what has now become known as *asymmetric* cryptography. Ralph Merkle described the same concept, at the same time (with a different algorithm), but his paper was, unfortunately, rejected as "uninteresting."

digest string of data of specific length, calculated from a file or message, in such a way that there is a high probability that any change to the original will result in a change to the digest. Usually part of a *digital signature*. Also known as hash or message digest. See also *cryptographic checksum*.

digital forensics sometimes known as digital forensic research or digital forensic science, this has recently become the umbrella term for all forms of research and analysis of computers and computer use directed at obtaining evidence of intrusion, attack, or wrongdoing. The First Digital Forensic Research Workshop defined digital forensic science as "[t]he use of scientifically derived and proven methods toward the preservation, collection, validation, identification, analysis, interpretation, documentation and presentation of digital evidence derived from digital sources for the purpose of facilitating or furthering the reconstruction of events found to be criminal, or helping to anticipate unauthorized actions shown to be disruptive to planned operations." Three major fields of digital forensics are *computer forensics, forensic programming,* and *network forensics.*

digital signature piece of information generated by *cryptographic* methods, whereby it can be demonstrated that an original message or file has not been deliberately altered or accidentally corrupted, and that the *identity* of the originator of the file can be *authenticated*

Digital Signature Algorithm (DSA) *asymmetric cryptographic algorithm* that produces a *digital signature* in the form of a pair of large numbers. Used in the *Digital Signature Standard.*

Digital Signature Standard (DSS) U.S. government standard that specifies the *Digital Signature Algorithm* (DSA)

digital watermarking computing techniques for inseparably embedding unobtrusive marks or labels as bits in digital data—text, graphics, images, video, or audio—and for detecting or extracting the marks later. The set of embedded bits (the digital watermark) is sometimes hidden, usually imperceptible, and always intended to be unobtrusive. Depending on the particular technique used, digital watermarking can assist in proving ownership, controlling duplication, tracing distribution, ensuring data integrity, and performing other functions to protect intellectual property rights. See also *steganography*.

direct action virus *virus* that immediately loads itself into memory, infects other files, and then unloads itself from memory

dirty power electrical utility power that is damaging to computers or other delicate electronic equipment. Spikes, brownouts, voltage significantly higher or lower than normal, or line noise can all cause problems of varying severity and are collectively known as "power hits."

disaster plan synonymous with *contingency plan*

disaster recovery plan (DRP) plan and preparations directed toward the resumption of business and the recovery of systems after catastrophic loss of important systems. A disaster recovery plan is generally concerned with longer time frames than a *business continuity plan*. Sometimes also referred to as a business resumption plan.

disclaimer The content of this Web page or book (if I've managed to sell it) is distributed on an "as is" basis, without surety, warranty, or assurance of any kind as to accuracy of content, quality of writing, punctuation, spelling, grammar, usefulness of the ideas presented, merchantability, liability, correctness or readability of concepts, or correspondence of (a) the definitions with the actual terms used, (ii) domain

name references in the URL (if any) with the actual
site used, and (4) any reference link with where the
link ends up. Illustrations may have been originally
necessary to understand this material: neither the
author nor the ISP accept any responsibility for the
fact that ASCII doesn't support them. Any resem-
blance of the author or his or her likeness or name
to any person, living or dead, or their heirs or
assigns (even if grandchildren), is coincidental; all
references to people, places, or events have been or
should have been fictionalized or at least randomly
chosen from the Quesnel phone directory and may
or may not have any factual basis, even if reported as
authentic. Similarities to existing works of fact, reference, art, literature, song, dance, puppetry, reality
television program, radio talk show, random conversation, or movie scripts is pure fluke. References
have been chosen at random from the author's own
written works (for purposes of self-promotion) or
fertile imagination. Neither the author(s) nor the
publisher shall have any liability whatever to any
person, corporation, animal (whether feral or
domesticated), mineral, vegetable, or other corporeal,
incorporeal, or supracorporeal entity with respect to
any loss, damage, misunderstanding, puzzlement, or
death from choking with laughter (I wish) or
apoplexy (more likely) at or due to, respectively, the
contents; that is caused or is alleged to be caused by
any party, whether directly or indirectly due to the
information or lack of information that may or may
not be found in this alleged work. No representation is made as to the correctness of the IP address
or date of publication as our Pentium isn't good

with numbers and errors of spelling and usage are attributable solely to bugs in the spelling and grammar checker in Microsoft Word even though the author does not use it. If sold without a header, this message will be shorter than those sold with a header. Slightly higher west of the Rockies. (The elevation, dummy, not the number of entries.) You do not own this page or book, but have acquired only a revocable non-exclusive licence to read the material contained herein. You may not read it aloud to any third party, regardless of any ability or inability of that third party to read it for themselves. This disclaimer is held to be valid under the laws of wherever I can best make it stick. This disclaimer is a copyrighted work of Robert M. Slade, first published in 2004, and is distributed "as is," without guarantee, warranty, or attestation as to quality of humour, trenchancy of critique, sharpness of scorn, or aptness of jape. Any similarity to any book disclaimer by Jef Raskin is purest accident.

disclosure (1) the act of providing access to specific information, usually without restriction
(2) relating to a philosophical debate about the value or necessity of making information about security *vulnerabilities* or *exploits* publicly available. Proponents of *full disclosure* would state that the information, including full details and possibly working exploit code to demonstrate the problem, needs to be made available to everyone to ensure that anyone charged with security provision has access to it, and to force vendors to face up to the fact that the problem exists. Proponents of non-disclosure insist that making information available means that it is made

available to those who would use it to attack systems. Most would recommend some form of partial disclosure, such as making the information available to the vendor for a month before publishing a warning about the existence of the problem. See also *limited disclosure, delayed disclosure,* and *security by obscurity.*

discretionary access control (DAC) means of restricting access to *objects* based on the identity and need-to-know of the user, process, and/or groups to which they belong. The controls are discretionary in the sense that a *subject* with a certain access permission is capable of passing that permission (perhaps indirectly) on to any other subject. Compare *mandatory access control.*

disinfection in *virus* work, the term can mean either the disabling of a virus' ability to operate, the removal of virus code, or the return of the system to a state identical to that prior to *infection.* Since these definitions can differ substantially in practice, discussions of the ability to disinfect an infected system can be problematic. Disinfection is the means users generally prefer to use in dealing with virus infections, but the safest means of dealing with an infection is to delete all infected *objects* and replace them with safe files from *backup.*

disk compression real-time compression and decompression of files on disk to effectively increase disk space. (Disk compression programs typically promise to double the size of the hard disk and are sometimes known as disk doublers.) Because compression is a form of encryption, scanning a compressed disk without the compression software running will typically hide *viruses* and other *malware* from a *scanner*. Disk compression is less of an issue of late given the drop in prices for large capacity disks.

Distributed Denial of Service (DDoS) distributed denial of service is almost universally referred to by its acronym, *DDoS*

DNS spoofing assuming the DNS (Domain Name Service) name of another system by either corrupting the name service cache of a victim system, or by compromising a domain name server for a valid domain

DMZ de-militarized zone, originally an area between two opposing armies or nations, not used by either side, and stripped of any cover to avoid penetration attempts by either side. (Similar to "no man's land" in World War I.) Now frequently used to describe the unused or unimportant area, physical or logical, between two layers of control in a *defence in depth* system. In particular, a *firewall* architecture where internal company networks are separated from publicly accessible servers, such as Web servers, which are themselves separated from the public Internet by another firewall.

DoD Trusted Computer System Evaluation Criteria (TCSEC) document published by the United States National Computer Security Center containing a uniform set of basic requirements and evaluation classes for assessing degrees of *assurance* in the effectiveness of hardware and software security controls built into systems. These criteria were intended for use in the design and evaluation of systems that would process and/or store sensitive or classified data. This document is United States Government Standard Department of Defense (DoD) 5200.28-STD and is frequently referred to as "The Orange Book." It was one of the standards that went into the production of the *Common Criteria*.

domain the unique context (e.g., access control parameters) in which a program is operating; in effect, the set of *objects* a *subject* has the ability to access. Should not be confused with the domain names used in Internet addressing. See *process* and *subject*.

dominate security level S1 is said to dominate security level S2 if the hierarchical classification of S1 is greater than or equal to that of S2, and the nonhierarchical categories of S1 include all those of S2 as a subset

dongle portable, physical, electronic device that is required to be attached to a computer to enable a particular software program to run. A form of *authentication token*.

DoS see *denial of service*

DOS Disk Operating System. Generally, any computer operating system, although currently often used as shorthand for Microsoft's MS-DOS or the related PC-DOS and DR-DOS. Not to be confused with DoS (*denial of service*).

dropper program, not itself infected, that will install a *virus* on a computer system. Virus authors often use droppers to seed their creations *in the wild*, particularly in the case of *boot sector infectors*. The term *injector* may refer to a dropper that installs a virus only in memory.

DSA see *Digital Signature Algorithm*

DSS see *Digital Signature Standard*

DTLS See *Descriptive Top-Level Specification*

dual homed host system that has two or more network interfaces, each of which is connected to a different network. In firewall configurations, a dual homed host usually acts to block or filter some or all of the traffic trying to pass between the networks. Sometimes called dual homed gateway.

dual infector see *multipartite*

due care required, just, proper, and sufficient care, so far as the circumstances demand; prudent. The absence of negligence. That degree of care a prudent person can be expected to exercise to avoid harm that is reasonably foreseeable if such care is not taken.

due diligence proof (usually documented) that due care has been exercised

dumpster diving practice of collecting and analysing garbage from a company installation to retrieve confidential data, especially security compromising information. (Dumpster is an American term for what is elsewhere called a skip.) In industrial espionage, the same activity is known as a "trash cover."

DWIM the opcode, not yet implemented on any known computer, that will resolve all problems; i.e., "Do What I Mean"

E

e-mail or email use email. I've studied the various telecom dictionaries, and they are about equally split. However, net and tech users (aside from *B1FF*) avoid extraneous characters (and, indeed, any extra characters at all). (If you do not know that email is "electronic mail," sending text-based messages through store and forward computer network systems, you shouldn't be reading this book.)

easter egg undocumented function in a program, generally intended as a *prank* on or treat for frequent users. Easter eggs range greatly in scope from mildly amusing error messages to the full implementation of a kind of flight simulator that appeared in one version of Microsoft's Excel spreadsheet program. Opinion regarding easter eggs varies, from those who see them as simply harmless jokes to those who consider the more complex inclusions to be *trojan horses*. In general, however, the practice of including easter eggs and other undocumented code in programs is detrimental to strict security. (OK, yes, this glossary is full of easter eggs.)

eavesdropping passive wiretapping done secretly, without the knowledge of the originator or the intended recipients of the communication

ECB see *electronic codebook*

economy of mechanism principle that each security mechanism should be designed to be as simple as possible, so the mechanism can be correctly implemented, can be implemented in most situations, and so that it can be verified that the operation of the mechanism enforces the containing system's *security policy*

EICAR European Institute of Computer Anti-Virus Research. See also *EICAR Standard Antivirus Test File*.

EICAR Standard Antivirus Test File In conjunction with several antivirus software companies, EICAR has developed a test file for antivirus software. This text file consists of one line of 68 printable characters; if saved as EICAR.COM, it can be executed and displays the message "EICAR-STANDARD-ANTIVIRUS-TEST-FILE!" This provides an easily reproducible executable file that many antiviral developers have agreed to detect with their programs. It thus affords a safe and simple way of testing whether an antiviral scanner is operating without using a real virus. The actual string is:

X5O!P%@AP[4\PZX54(P^)7CC)7}$EICAR-STANDARD-ANTIVIRUS-TEST-FILE!$H+H*

El Gamal algorithm unpatented algorithm for *asymmetric cryptography*, invented in 1985 by Taher El Gamal, that is based on the difficulty of calculating discrete logarithms and can be used for both *encryption* and *digital signatures*

electronic codebook (ECB) *block cipher* mode that uses no feedback. Identical blocks of *plaintext* are transformed into identical *ciphertext* blocks. Considered the weakest form of block cipher.

electronic emission security measures taken to protect transmissions or *emanations*, particularly inadvertent and inherent, from interception and electronic analysis. The most famous form was *TEMPEST*.

electronic vaulting transfer of data to a remote facility (for storage purposes) via a communications channel

elliptic curve cryptography (ECC) type of *asymmetric cryptography* based on mathematics of groups that are defined by the points on a curve. The most efficient implementation of ECC is claimed to be stronger per bit of key length than any other known form of asymmetric cryptography. ECC can be used to define an algorithm for key agreement that is an analog of the *Diffie-Hellman*, and an algorithm for digital signature that is an analog of the Digital Signature Algorithm.

emanations see *compromising emanations*

embedded system system that performs or controls a function, either in whole or in part, as an integral element of a larger system or subsystem

emergency sudden, generally unexpected event that does or could do harm to people, the environment, resources, property, or institutions

emergency plan synonymous with *contingency plan*

emission security protection resulting from all measures taken to deny unauthorized persons information of value that might be derived from intercept and from an analysis of *compromising emanations* from systems

Encapsulating Security Payload (ESP) Internet *IPsec* protocol (RFC 2406) designed to provide a mix of security services—especially data confidentiality service—in the Internet Protocol. See *also Authentication Header*. ESP may be used alone, in combination with the IPsec AH protocol, or in a nested fashion with tunnelling. The ESP header is encapsulated by the IP header, and the ESP header encapsulates either the upper layer protocol header (transport mode) or an IP header (tunnel mode). ESP can provide confidentiality service, origin authentication service, connectionless data integrity service, an anti-replay service, and limited traffic flow confidentiality.

encrypted virus *virus* whose code begins with a decryption algorithm and continues with scrambled or encrypted code for the remainder of the virus. Each time it infects, a different encryption key is chosen to avoid providing a consistent scan string to use as a *signature*. Through this method, the virus tries to avoid detection by antivirus software. The term "encrypted virus" is a loose one, and seldom used in the antiviral research community. More rigorously, the term "self-encryption" is used, as a specific type of *polymorphic* activity.

encryption process of transforming a message (or *plaintext*) into apparently random noise (or *ciphertext*) such that the message can be extracted by those in possession of an appropriate *key*, but is difficult or impossible to extract by unauthorized parties. Also, the process of placing a coffin in a mausoleum—GJS per ME.

encryption algorithm set of logical or mathematical rules for rendering data unintelligible, through a series of transformations to the normal representation of the information, usually controlled by a *key* or *cryptovariable*. See also *cryptographic algorithm.*

end-to-end encryption protection of information passed in a telecommunications system by cryptographic means, from point of origin to point of destination, provided by encrypting data when it leaves its source, leaving it encrypted while it passes through any intermediate computers (such as routers), and decrypting only when the data arrives at the intended destination. When two points are separated by multiple communication links that are connected by one or more intermediate relays, end-to-end encryption enables the source and destination systems to protect their communications without depending on the intermediate systems to provide the protection. The alternate system for communications encryption is *link encryption.*

Endorsed Tools List (ETL) list of formal verification tools endorsed by the NCSC (National Computer Security Center) for the development of systems with high levels of trust. U.S. government and military.

entrapment deliberate planting of apparent flaws in a system for the purpose of detecting attempted penetrations. See *honeypot* and *pseudo flaw.* This technical definition of entrapment should not be confused with the legal sense of the word, which is the specific incitement to a particular illegal act.

environment aggregate of external procedures, conditions, and *objects* that affect the development, operation, and maintenance of a system

ephemeral key key that is relatively short-lived. See *session key*

erasure process by which a signal recorded on magnetic media is removed. Complete erasure is usually accomplished by applying a magnetic field to the media. Deleting a file, particularly under a desktop operating system, does not necessarily erase the contents of the file.

Eris the Greek goddess of Chaos, Discord, Confusion, and Things You Know Not Of; the connection to security is obvious. See also *Sisyphus the Perplexed*.

error log file created by the operating system that may be useful for review as part of the audit process

escalation increasing the level of reporting or action in regard to an *event* or *incident*, particularly as evidence accumulates that the scope or significance of the incident is greater than originally thought

ESP see *Encapsulating Security Payload*

ethical hacker the way the term is used, an "ethical hacker" is simply a *penetration tester*, one who assesses the security of an installation, or, in the most generic use, an IT security auditor. Since we know what a penetration tester is, and the term "ethical hacker" is both emotionally loaded and not terribly clear, use of the term should be avoided.

ethics principles of conduct governing an individual or group

evacuation (1) controlled movement of personnel from a site under threat to a safe location
(2) no, we aren't interested in any nursing jokes

Evaluated Products List (EPL) list of equipment, hardware, software, and/or firmware that have been evaluated against, and found to be technically compliant with, the U.S. Department of Defense *TCSEC* by the NCSC (National Computer Security Center) at a particular level of trust. U.S. government and military.

event any untoward or potentially negative single occurrence. A collection of events may make up an *incident*.

evil twin wireless LAN access point, set up to appear to be an Internet access hotspot. When a user connects to the site, the evil twin can sniff all traffic, collecting information such as passwords and credit card numbers. Often known as a rogue access point.

exception error condition generated by hardware or software. Developers must consider possible errors and exceptions to normal operation, and provide exception handling, often through special software modules known as exception handlers. Failure to address exceptions may result in *bugs* such as *buffer overflows*. Less critical types of exception handling may involve protection of data integrity, such as *sanity checking*. (Thanks, Fred.)

executive state one of several states in which a system may operate and the only one in which certain privileged instructions may be executed. Such instructions cannot be executed when the system is operating in other (user) states. Synonymous with supervisor state.

exploit specific *attack* or *vulnerability* used to take advantage of a particular *loophole* or weakness in security measures. Very similar in meaning to *exposure*, and sometimes the two terms are used synonymously.

exploitable channel any information channel that is usable or detectable by *subjects* external to the trusted computing base whose purpose is to violate the security policy of the system. See *covert channel*.

exposure particular weakness or *vulnerability* to a specific *attack*. Also, the measure of *risk* to a particular *threat*.

external label visible marking on the outside or cover of media that reflects the classification and sensitivity of the information resident within media. See also *internal label* and *label*.

F

fail over design or condition where the failure or overloading of a component or system transfers demand or function to another, usually identical, unit. Systems designed for fail over are usually arranged with multiple units in sequence.

fail safe automatic protection of programs and/or processing systems to maintain safety when a hardware or software failure is detected in a system. The overriding principle is that failure of one part or component will not result in the failure or termination of the system as a whole. In terms of security, fail safe is sometimes seen as a tendency to fail open: failure of access controls, for example, will ensure that access continues to be granted—sometimes even to those to whom it should not be granted. Compare with *fail secure*.

fail secure in the event of a failure of a part or component of the system, the system itself will terminate or fail, rather than suffer any loss of security. Compare with *fail safe*.

fail soft pertaining to the selective termination of affected nonessential processing when a hardware or software failure is detected in a system. The term "graceful degradation" is sometimes used.

failure access unauthorized and usually inadvertent access to data resulting from a hardware or software failure in the system

failure control method used to detect and provide *fail safe* or *fail soft* recovery from hardware and software failures in a system

false acceptance error condition where a *subject, object,* or operation is accepted as valid, when it should have been rejected as invalid, incorrect, or a *compromise* of the *security policy.* Also known as a Type II error. See also *false rejection, false negative,* and *crossover error rate.*

false acceptance rate (FAR) measure of the accuracy of a security safeguard, expressed as a proportion or percentage of the number of *false acceptance,* or Type II, errors against the total number of events. See also *crossover error rate.*

false alarm see *false rejection* and *false positive*

false negative there are two types of false reports from *antiviral* software. A false negative report is when an antiviral reports no viral activity or presence, when there is a *virus* present. References to false negatives are usually only made in technical reports. Most people simply refer to an antiviral "missing" a virus. A false negative is more generally known in the security community as a *false acceptance,* or a Type II error.

false positive the second kind of false report an *antiviral* can make is to report the activity or presence of a *virus* when there is, in fact, no virus. False positive has come to be widely used among those who know about viral and antiviral programs. Very few use the analogous term, *false alarm.* A false positive is more generally known in the security community as a *false rejection*, or a Type I error.

false rejection error condition where a *subject*, *object*, or operation that should be accepted as valid is rejected as invalid, incorrect, or a *compromise* of the *security policy*. Also known as a Type I error. See also *false acceptance*, *false positive*, and *crossover error rate*.

false rejection rate (FRR) measure of the accuracy of a security safeguard, expressed as a proportion or percentage of the number of *false rejection*, or Type I, errors against the total number of events. See also *crossover error rate*.

fan out in terms of *incident response*, a system whereby each person notified of the incident has the responsibility to call additional personnel, thus speeding the contact process. It should be noted that provision should be made for *redundancy* in such a system to prevent situations in which a failure at one point would prevent contact of an entire segment of the team. See also *call tree*.

fast burner *virus*, usually email or network based, that spreads around the world within hours. *Melissa* and *Loveletter* are considered the prototypical fast burners. The original *Internet Worm* and *Code Red* certainly spread around the world within hours, but only created tens or hundreds of thousands of copies, whereas true fast burners are generally measured in the millions.

fast infector originally, this referred to a *virus* that infected any program file opened, even if the program was not executed. Later viruses were able to search for and infect files even if they were not opened, so the distinction became meaningless. This term is seldom used in virus research any longer.

FAT virus see *cluster virus*

fault condition that causes a device or system component to fail to perform in a required manner

fault tolerance ability of a system or component to continue normal operation despite the presence of hardware or software faults. Also the number of faults a system or component can withstand before normal operation is impaired.

fetch protection system-provided restriction to prevent a program from accessing data in another user's segment of storage

File Allocation Table (FAT) MS-DOS specific term for that area of system information on the disk that refers to the physical areas of the disk that are taken up by files or portions of files. Certain viral programs are said to take over a file pointer without affecting directory information by manipulating FAT information. This is not quite accurate, and most researchers tend to prefer the use of the term *cluster virus* or *system virus*.

file infector *virus* that attaches itself to, or associates itself with, a file, usually a program file. File infectors most often append or prepend themselves to regular program files, or overwrite program code. The file infector class is often also used to refer to programs that do not physically attach to files but associate themselves with program filenames. See also *system virus* and *companion virus.*

file protection aggregate of all processes and procedures in a system designed to inhibit unauthorized access to, contamination of, or elimination of a file

file security means by which access to computer files is limited to authorized users only

filter program that processes an input data stream into an output data stream in some well-defined way. This has implications for various security applications, most particularly in terms of *firewalls.*

filtering router internetwork router that selectively prevents the passage of data packets according to a *security policy.* A filtering router may be used as a *firewall* or part of a firewall. A router usually receives a packet from a network and decides where to forward it on a second network. A filtering router does the same, but first decides whether the packet should be forwarded at all, according to specific security policy. The policy is implemented by rules (packet filters) loaded into the router. The rules mostly involve values of data packet control fields, especially source and destination addresses, protocol fields, and port numbers.

firewall secured system passing and examining traffic between an internal trusted network and an external untrusted network such as the Internet. Firewalls can be used to detect, prevent, or mitigate certain types of network *attack.* See also *application level gateway* and *proxy server.*

firmware computer programs and data stored in hardware—typically in read-only memory (ROM) or programmable read-only memory (PROM)—such that the programs and data cannot be dynamically written or modified during execution of the programs. An important exception is flash EEPROM (Electrically Erasable Programmable Read-Only Memory), which can be rewritten in some circumstances. See also *BIOS*.

FIRST see *Forum of Incident Response and Security Teams*

flag (1) in data transmission, an indicator, such as a signal, symbol, character, or digit, used for identification (2) a variable or quantity that can take one of two values; a bit, particularly one that is used to indicate one of two outcomes or is used to control which of two things is to be done

flame to post an email message intended to insult and provoke. Sometimes, flames are sent deliberately to start an argument or "flame war," an action known as trolling.

flaw defect in the design of software, as opposed to a *bug*, which is an error in implementation

flaw hypothesis methodology systems analysis and penetration technique in which specifications and documentation for the system are analyzed and then flaws in the system are hypothesized. The list of hypothesized flaws is then priorized on the basis of the estimated probability that a flaw exists and, assuming a flaw does exist, on the ease of exploiting the flaw, and on the extent of control or compromise the flaw would provide. The prioritized list is used to direct a penetration attack against the system. This is similar to scenario based planning.

flow control see *information flow control*

forensic programming originally from the field of computer *virus* research, forensic programming involves the analysis of code for evidence of intent, program identity, or authorship. Outside of virus research, forensic is often referred to as code analysis, although code analysis may be limited to analysis of source code, whereas forensic programming frequently deals with object code when object code is the only evidence available. The broader field, examining all forms of code, is becoming known as software forensics. One of the major divisions of *digital forensics*.

formal access approval documented approval by a data owner to allow access to a particular category of information

formal proof complete and convincing mathematical argument, presenting the full logical justification for each proof step, and for the truth of a theorem or set of theorems

formal security policy model mathematically precise statement of a *security policy*. To be adequately precise, such a model must represent the initial state of a system, the way in which the system progresses from one state to another, and a definition of a "secure" state of the system. To be acceptable as a basis for a *TCB* (Trusted Computing Base), the model must be supported by a formal proof that if the initial state of the system satisfies the definition of a "secure" state and if all assumptions required by the model hold, then all future states of the system will be secure. Some formal modelling techniques include state transition models, denotational semantics models, and algebraic specification models. See *Bell-La Padula* model and *security policy model*.

Formal Top-Level Specification (FTLS) top-level specification that is written in a formal mathematical language to allow theorems showing the correspondence of the system specification to its formal requirements to be hypothesized and formally proven

formal verification process of using formal proofs to demonstrate the consistency between a formal specification of a system and a formal security policy model (design verification), or between the formal specification and its high-level program implementation (implementation verification)

format structure of a data file, or a storage device or medium containing information, and particularly the command to prepare such media for holding information. Because issuing a format command generally results in the loss of ability to retrieve files previously stored, it is generally felt that the format command is an effective means of erasure of data. In fact, in many situations (particularly under Microsoft Windows), the format command does not erase data at all. On other platforms (such as UNIX), the format command may take other options, some of which may support functions such as *overwriting* delete.

Forum of Incident Response and Security Teams (FIRST) international consortium of CSIRTs (Computer Security Incident Response Teams) that work together to handle computer security incidents and promote preventive activities. FIRST was founded in 1990 and, as of September 1999 had nearly 70 members spanning the globe. It attempts to provide members with technical information, tools, methods, assistance, and guidance; coordinate proactive liaison activities and analytical support; encourage development of quality products and services; improve national and international information security for government, private industry, academia, and the individual; and enhance the image and status of the CSIRT community.

forward error correction system of error control for data transmission wherein the receiving device has the capability to detect and correct any character or code block that contains fewer than a predetermined number of symbols in error. *Hamming code* is an example.

forward secrecy for a key agreement protocol based on *asymmetric cryptography*, the property that ensures that a *session key* derived from a set of long-term *public* and *private keys* will not be compromised if one of the private keys is compromised in the future. The term "perfect forward secrecy" is frequently used in this regard, but is not defined precisely. The term "public-key forward secrecy" (suggested by Hilarie

Orman) is probably more accurate, but, because of the various terms using the phrase "forward secrecy" it is the phrase defined in this glossary. There are also discussions of "backward" security, but there does not seem to be agreement on whether this refers to a weakening of a private key if the derived session key is compromised, or if a compromise of one session key weakens session keys used previously. *Symmetric* systems probably do not have any similar property, since compromise of the key compromises the entire system.

fraud intentional perversion of truth for the purpose of obtaining some benefit or resource from the person in control of it

freeware software to which the author or developer still retains *copyright* (unlike *public domain*), but for the use of which there is no charge (unlike *shareware* or *commercial* software). There are sometimes restrictions on the use or distribution of freeware. See also *open source*.

front end intermediary computer that does setup and filtering for another (usually more powerful but less friendly) machine (a back end). Also, software that provides an interface to another program behind it.

front-end security filter security filter, which could be implemented in hardware or software, that is logically separated from the remainder of the system to protect the system's integrity

ftp ftp has little to do with security at all, it has just come to be such a very common term among those who work on the Internet that we use it a number of times without ever defining it. ftp (almost always written in lowercase: despite the fact that it is an acronym, the usage stems from the fact that UNIX programs are generally lowercase) is the file transfer protocol of the Internet: the way to copy files between computers. It is often used as a verb, as in "Where do I find the latest copy of DISKSE-CURE?" "Oh, you can ftp it from urvax." A computer set up to provide files for all callers from anywhere on the Internet is known as an "ftp site": more commonly now called an anonymous ftp site, since most sites do not require the use of an established account. See *anonymous login*.

full backup *backup* process that makes a copy of all data and/or software on a system, or such a copy. A full backup is the only item needed for complete system restoration, but takes the longest to perform. See also *differential backup* and *incremental backup*.

full disclosure extreme form of *vulnerability disclosure* that holds that information about any vulnerability should be released to the general public with no restrictions. Full disclosure may also hold that announcements of vulnerabilities should be accompanied by working *exploit* code, possibly demonstrating the most dangerous possible exploit. While full disclosure is sometimes advocated by members of the security research community, the AV virus research community has always held that notification of the existence of viruses is desirable, but distribution of exploit code (working viruses) is to be extremely limited.

functional testing segment of security testing in which the advertised security mechanisms of the system are tested, under operational conditions, for correct operation

G

gap analysis examination of discrepancies between security requirements and controls or safeguards in place

garbage collection particular class of strategies for dynamically but transparently reallocating computer memory in running applications. One such strategy involves periodically scanning all the data in memory: locations with useless data items are then made available so the memory they occupy can be recycled and used for another purpose. If the data is not cleared from these locations before reallocation, the information may be made available to processes or users despite normal access restrictions.

General Public Virus pejorative or ironic name for some versions of the GNU (Gnu's Not UNIX) project *copyleft* or General Public License (GPL), which requires that any *open source* tools or applications incorporating copylefted code must be source-distributed on the same counter-commercial terms as GNU material. Thus, it is alleged that the copyleft *"infects"* software generated with GNU tools, which may in turn infect other software that reuses any of its code.

generic (1) *activity monitoring* and *change detection* software, since they look for viral-like activity rather than specific *virus signatures*, are often referred to as generic *antivirals*. *Heuristic scanners* are often included since they are a special case of activity monitors. (2) a virus *scan string* that matches more than one virus. The usefulness of generic signatures is sometimes questioned.

(3) the use of error recovery or heuristic techniques for *disinfection*.

germ like bacterium, this is another term for a viral program that does not directly attach to programs. Usage obscure.

Get A Life! way of suggesting that the target is taking some obscure issue too seriously. It is generally held that the majority of *blackhats*, and particularly the obsessive *wannabe* script kiddies, do not Have A Life.

GIGO acronym for "Garbage In, Garbage Out," an explanation that systems behave improperly when given imperfect input or are otherwise mistreated in some way. Also commonly used to describe failures in human decision making due to faulty, incomplete, or imprecise data. The original statement of this premise, although not so concise, goes all the way back to Charles Babbage: "On two occasions I have been asked (by members of Parliament!), 'Pray, Mr. Babbage, if you put into the machine wrong figures, will the right answers come out?' I am not able rightly to apprehend the kind of confusion of ideas that could provoke such a question." More recently, the expression "Garbage In, Gospel Out" has become a sardonic comment on the tendency human beings have to put excessive trust in computerized data or systems. See also *Trust the Machines*.

go bag in emergency planning, a bag, pack, or other single container holding resources necessary for someone to operate in the initial stages of an emergency and for some hours thereafter. See also *battle box*.

goat see *bait*

gold standard the *best practice* in describing your standard, if you want people to buy into it

granularity expression of the relative size of a data *object*; e.g., protection at the file level is considered coarse granularity, whereas protection at record or field level is considered to be of a finer granularity

green machine computer or peripheral device that has been designed and built to military specifications for field equipment (that is, to withstand mechanical shock, extremes of temperature and humidity, and so forth). Comes from the olive-drab uniform paint used for military equipment.

guard processor that provides a filter between two disparate systems operating at different security levels or between a user terminal and a database to filter out data the user is not authorized to access

guest login see *anonymous login*

guideline usually a part of a security *policy*, a guideline is a suggestion or recommendation as opposed to a required *standard*. A guideline may also be informative, such as a list of "*best practices*" or an evaluation criteria.

H

hacker originally, the term meant one who was skilled in the use of computer systems, particularly if that skill was acquired in an exploratory manner. Later, the term evolved to be applied to those, skilled or unskilled, who break security systems. Actually, you can generally determine people's level of technical expertise by how they use the term. A person who uses "hacker" for "expert" is someone who really does advanced technical work. Someone who uses "hacker" as meaning a bad guy may have a technical background of some type, or a technical job, but usually is nowhere near the cutting edge.

hacktivism system penetration or corruption with a political or social intent. The term is considered slang, and is not carefully defined, but is generally acceptable.

Hamming code error-detecting and -correcting binary code used in data transmission that can detect all single and double bit errors and can correct all single bit errors. Hamming codes must satisfy $k=m(m-1)$ and $m=n-k$, where n is the number of bits in the block, k is the number of information bits in the block, and m is the number of check bits in the block. See also *forward error correction* code.

handshaking procedure dialogue between two entities (e.g., a user and a computer, a computer and another computer, or a program and another program) used for *identification* and *authentication* of the entities to one another

Hanlon's Razor "Never attribute to malice that which can be adequately explained by stupidity."

hardcopy information or data in some fixed media. Hardcopy generally refers to a medium that is difficult to modify, and usually in human-readable form, such as printed on paper. Hardcopy may be the preferred form of *backup* in cases where the data may need to outlast the lifetime of certain forms of storage technology. Hardcopy is also usually preferred in many situations for evidentiary purposes, especially in regard to presentation in courts of law.

hash see *digest*

hash function algorithm that computes a value based on a data object (such as a message or file; usually variable length; possibly very large), thereby mapping the data object to a smaller data object (the *hash result*) that is usually a fixed-size value. A *checksum* is a very simplistic hash function. A good hash function is such that the results of applying the function to a set of values in the domain will be evenly distributed (and apparently at random) over the range. The kind of hash function needed for security applications is called a *cryptographic* hash function, an algorithm for which it is computationally infeasible to find either (a) a data object that maps to a prespecified hash result (the "one-way" property), or (b) two data objects that map to the same hash result (the "collision-free" property).

hash result output of a hash function, also known as a hash value. The output produced by a hash function upon processing a message or file.

help desk most common name for that person or office in an organization where users are directed for technical support or assistance. Help desk personnel should receive at least basic security education and training, since they will likely receive the first reports of anomalies that may indicate an *attack* or other security problem.

heuristic in *antiviral* terms, the examination of program code for functions known to be associated with viral activity. In most cases, this is similar to *activity monitoring* but without actually executing the program; in other cases, code is run under some type of emulation. There has also been a heuristic disinfection program that attempted to remove viral infections by examination of unknown code. In more general computing discussions, heuristic may have a meaning similar to algorithm, or it may relate to shortcuts to solutions taken on the basis of a "best guess." Thus, a *dictionary attack* may be seen as a heuristic type of *brute force* attack.

heuristic scanner *antiviral* program that attempts to detect new or unknown *viruses* or *malware* by the examination of program code for functions known to be associated with viral or malicious activity

hijacking *attack* whereby an active, established session is intercepted and used by the attacker

HMAC keyed hash (RFC 2104) that can be based on any iterated cryptographic hash. The goals of HMAC are to use available *cryptographic hash functions* without modification (particularly functions that perform well in software and for which software is freely and widely available), to preserve the original performance of the selected hash without significant degradation, to use and handle *keys* in a simple way, to have a well-understood cryptographic analysis of the strength of the mechanism based on reasonable assumptions about the underlying hash function, and to enable easy replacement of the hash function in case a faster or stronger hash is found or required. There does not appear to be an official expansion for the acronym HMAC. It may be similar to Hash-keyed Message *Authentication* Code: the title of the RFC (Request For Comments) is "Keyed Hashing for Message Authentication."

hoax literally, of course, a joke, fraud, or other form of spoofing. The term "hoax" has developed a specific technical meaning in virus research in reference to a form of chain letter, carrying a false warning of a non-existent virus. Originally (1988) referred to in the research community as a metavirus, this type of activity was more widely seen in the late 1990s in the "Good Times," "Penpals," "Budweiser Frogs," "Jesus Loves You," and "SULFNBK.EXE" hoaxes. Hoaxes are characterized by a lack of technical detail and valid contact information, references to false authorities, warnings of extreme damage that the putative virus will cause, all uppercase "SHOUTING" and exclamation marks in the text, and, frequently, statements that the virus is too new or spreading too rapidly for legitimate virus researchers to know anything about. The one universal factor in hoaxes is the attempt to have the reader forward the message to all friends, relatives,

and contacts, which is, of course, the viral component: the hoax message uses the user to retransmit
and spread. Recent writings about hoaxes often
make use of the term *meme* or meme virus.

honeypot system, or portion of a system, deliberately
established to be enticing to an intruder or system
cracker. Honeypots generally have additional functionality and *intrusion detection systems* built into
them to gather information on the intruders. See
also *entrapment*.

host-based security technique of securing an individual
system from attack. Host-based security is operating
system and version dependent.

host to front-end protocol set of conventions governing
the format and control of data that are passed from a
host to a front-end machine

hot site standby site fully configured with compatible
computer and communications equipment, ready to
operate as soon as data can be loaded. Other than
fully redundant operation, the highest level provided
for in a *disaster recovery plan*. Some organizations
now refer to "immediate recovery." Compare with
cold site.

https when used as the protocol specifier in the first part of
a URL this term indicates the use of HTTP
enhanced by Secure Sockets Layer (SSL). It should
not be confused with S-HTTP (Secure HTTP).

hybrid encryption application of *cryptography* that combines two or more encryption algorithms, particularly a combination of *symmetric* and *asymmetric*

encryption. Asymmetric algorithms require more computation than equivalently strong symmetric ones. Thus, asymmetric encryption is not normally used for data confidentiality except in distributing symmetric keys in applications where the key data is usually short compared to the data it protects. Probably the most widely known example of a hybrid system is *PGP.*

Hybris most specialists would probably define Hybris as a *worm* rather than a *virus*, since it sends copies of itself as email attachments. Hybris will generally come in a message with a coy indication that the attachment is pornography. The attachment is often named with a .SCR extension. The extension is traditionally used to indicate screen savers, but the file format is the same as any normal executable Windows program. The notable feature of Hybris is that, when active, it checks for replacement and upgrade modules on the alt.comp.virus newsgroup. Other viruses, such as *Loveletter*, have attempted to establish such a modular extension function, but Hybris extended the concept further, and used an anonymous communications facility.

I

IBM compatible originally, hardware compatible with IBM mainframe systems, later hardware and/or software compatible with IBM mainframes or minicomputers. In the 1980s, the phrase came to be associated with compatibility with *ISA* and MS-DOS (and later Windows) systems.

ICMP Internet Control Message Protocol. Since these packets, as the name suggests, relate to various types of control information for the Internet, there are a number of Internet security implications.

ICMP flood *denial of service attack* that sends a host more ICMP (Internet Control Message Protocol) echo request ("ping") packets than the protocol implementation can handle

identification process that enables recognition of an entity by a system, generally by the use of unique machine-readable usernames

identity theft use of personal information to *impersonate* someone, usually for the purpose of fraud

impact extent to which an *incident* will affect operations or the overall organization. See *business impact analysis*.

impersonation synonymous with *spoofing*

implementation phase of the system development process in which the detailed specifications are translated into actual system components

in the clear not encrypted. See *cleartext* and *plaintext*.

in the wild initially a jargon reference to those *viruses* that have been released into, and successfully spread in, the normal computer user community and environment. It is used to distinguish those viral programs that are written and tested in a controlled research environment, without escaping, from those that are uncontrolled in the wild or in the field. (The term "itw" is sometimes also used, or "ItW" in specific reference to the list of common viruses known as the WildList.) The term is now also being used to refer to *vulnerabilities* discovered and *exploited* by *attackers* before being discovered by defenders or researchers.

incident occurrence that has been assessed as having an adverse effect on the security or performance of a system. Note that this definition is somewhat vague, particularly in regard to the level of assessment. Those from a law enforcement background tend to see incidents in terms of attacks with (potentially) identifiable intruders. Those from a systems administration or support background tend to see an incident as any anomaly in the system that might affect performance or service.

incident response reaction, generally by a pre-designated team, to a detrimental *incident*. At this time, incident response literature is primarily concerned with the collection and preservation of evidence in a manner appropriate for presentation in a court of law.

incomplete parameter checking system design flaw that results when all parameters have not been fully anticipated for accuracy and consistency, thus making the system vulnerable to penetration

incremental backup *backup* process that copies only data or changes since the last backup of any type, or such a copy. Incremental backup is the fastest form of backup, but restoration of the system requires the last *full backup*, and every incremental backup since. See also *differential backup*.

individual accountability ability to associate positively the identity of a user with the time, method, and degree of *access* to a system

infectable *object* to which *virus* code can attach or become associated with, in such a manner that invocation of the object will also invoke the virus

infection condition in which *virus* code has become attached to or associated with an *object* or system, in such a manner that invocation of the object or system will also invoke the virus. An infection, on a given system, does not take place until a virus has become active, reproduced, or made a change to the system. A user or system may receive a virus as a file transfer, virus infected piece of software, or email attachment, and not necessarily become infected. As long as a user does not invoke the virus, or a worm does not find a specific *vulnerability* to exploit, the infected file may remain dormant on the system, without the system itself becoming infected. However, a system may also be considered infected if the virus has either placed itself in a situation such that the operating system will activate it during a common occurrence (such as at boot time), or if a user is likely to call an infected, and commonly used, program. See also *disinfection*.

information flow analysis tracing the flow of specific information types through an information system to determine whether the controls applied to this information are appropriate

information flow control procedure to ensure that information transfers within a system are not made from a higher security level *object* to an object of a lower security level. See *covert channel*, *simple security property*, and **-property*. Synonymous with *data flow control* and *flow control*.

information label piece of information that accurately and completely represents the sensitivity of the data in a *subject* or *object*. More frequently just used as *label*.

information sensitivity relative worth of information to an organization. See also *classification*.

information system security measures and controls that protect a system against *denial of service* and unauthorized (accidental or intentional) disclosure, modification, or destruction of systems and data. System security includes consideration of all hardware and/or software functions, characteristics and/or features; operational procedures, accountability procedures, and access controls at the central computer facility, remote computer, and terminal facilities; management constraints; physical structures and devices; and personnel and communication controls needed to provide an acceptable level of risk for the system and for the data and information contained in the system. It includes the totality of security *safeguards* needed to provide an acceptable protection level for a system and for data handled by a system.

Information System Security Officer (ISSO) the person responsible to the *Designated Approving Authority* for ensuring that security is provided for and implemented throughout the life cycle of a system from the beginning of the concept development plan through its design, development, operation, maintenance, and secure disposal

initialization vector (IV) sequence of random bytes appended to the front of the *plaintext* before *encryption* by a *block cipher*, or used as a part of the first step in a block cipher procedure that uses some form of chaining. Use of the initialization vector eliminates the possibility of having the initial *ciphertext* block the same for any two messages. The concepts of *challenge/response, initialization vector, nonce,* and *salt* are closely related. Challenge/response is generally used in regard to password and authentication schemes, initialization vector to block ciphers, nonce to short automated network messages, and salt to password storage. Also known as initialization value.

infector program, not itself infected, that will place a *virus* in memory and render it active, without writing the virus to disk. Seldom used in antivirus research. See *dropper*.

insider attack *attack* involving an employee or other trusted individual, generally one with a higher than normal level of *access*

integrity sound, unimpaired, or perfect condition. Integrity is one of the *three pillars* of security.

integrity checking see *change detection*

intellectual property ideas, concepts, expressions, processes, or devices created by original thought and work and claimed by individuals or corporate entities under legal provisions. There are specific provisions for devices (patent), expressions (copyright), processes (trade secret), and perceptible and obvious design (trademark).

intellectual property rights right to that body of knowledge, ideas, or concepts produced by an entity that is claimed by that entity to be original and of quality and value

interdiction see *denial of service*

internal label marking of an item of information, to reflect the classification and sensitivity of the information, within the confines of the media containing the information

internal security controls hardware, firmware, and software features within a system that restrict access to resources (hardware, software, and data) to authorized *subjects* only (persons, programs, or devices)

International Data Encryption Algorithm (IDEA) *symmetric block cipher* that uses a 128-bit key and operates on 64-bit blocks

Internet Protocol security (IPsec) (1) the name of the IETF (Internet Engineering Task Force) working group that is specifying a security architecture (RFC 2401) and related protocols to provide security services for Internet Protocol traffic. IPsec is an Internet Protocol version 6 (IPv6) protocol suite, but will work under the current IPv4.

(2) a collective name for that architecture and set of protocols. The IPsec architecture specifies (a) security protocols (AH and ESP, the *Authentication Header* and *Encapsulating Security Payload*), (b) security associations (what they are, how they work, how they are managed, and associated processing), (c) key management (IKE), and (d) algorithms for authentication and encryption. The set of security services includes *access control* service, connectionless data *integrity* service, data origin *authentication* service, protection against replays (detection of the arrival of duplicate datagrams, within a constrained window), data *confidentiality* service, and limited traffic flow confidentiality.

Internet Security Association and Key Management Protocol (ISAKMP) Internet *IPsec* protocol (RFC 2408) to negotiate, establish, modify, and delete security associations, and to exchange key generation and *authentication* data, independent of the details of any specific key generation technique, key establishment protocol, *encryption* algorithm, or authentication mechanism.

Internet Worm also known as the UNIX Worm after the operating system it used, or the Morris Worm after the author, or, specifically, the Internet/Morris/ UNIX Worm, or sometimes simply the Worm, as the only one to be so capitalized. Launched in

November 1988, it spread to some three to four thousand machines connected to the Internet, wasting CPU cycles and clogging mail spools. It affected mail traffic (in particular) on the Internet as a whole for a few days and is probably the viral program most widely known to the general public prior to *Michelangelo, Melissa, Loveletter*, and *Code Red.*

intrusion *attacks* or attempted attacks from outside the security perimeter of a system

intrusion detection system (IDS) automated system for alerting operators to a penetration or other contravention of a *security policy*. Some intrusion detection systems may also have means for responding to a penetration by shutting down *access* or gathering more information on the intruder. See also *anomaly detection* and *network forensics*.

IP spoofing attack whereby an active, established session is intercepted and co-opted by the attacker by assuming the IP (Internet Protocol) numeric address, and usually redirecting the routing for that address. IP spoof attacks may occur after an *authentication* has been made, permitting the attacker to assume the role of an already authorized user. Primary protections against IP spoofing rely on *encryption* at the session or network layer. Also known as IP *hijacking* or IP splicing.

IPsec see *Internet Protocol security*

ISA Industry Standard Architecture, the name given by IBM to the basic structure of the IBM PC and XT computers, those referred to at the time as IBM or PC compatible. The designation is commonly held to apply to computers based on Intel 8088/8086/80x86/Pentium family processors, interrupt-based *BIOS boot* programming, and the associated bus, which is actually what ISA referred to, and is, ironically, the part of the machine that has undergone the greatest change. The ability of these computers to run the Microsoft MS-DOS and Windows operating systems, and the use of Intel CPUs, has also led to the use of the term "Wintel," although this architecture is also the most popular platform for those using the Linux operating system. The term does not have any specific security meanings, and is included here solely because Wintel computers play such a large factor in the overall computing environment that a number of system-specific details must be mentioned in this document.

Wintel is probably the more recognizable term, and ISA is really not completely accurate to describe architecture as it currently stands. On the other hand, Wintel is slang. On balance, I probably could have chosen to define either. So why choose ISA rather than Wintel as the entry to be fully defined? In the end, probably because it came first in the alphabet.

ISAKMP see *Internet Security Association and Key Management Protocol*

ISC² International Information Systems Security Certification Consortium (IISSCC), group responsible for the Certified Information Systems Security Professional (CISSP) and other designations. The group is generally abbreviated ISC2, or (ISC)2, or (ISC)^2, which are all usable in text or email, or, most properly, (ISC)², which cannot be represented in printable, text-only, characters. The organization has a Web site at *www.isc2.org*.

isolation containment of *subjects* and *objects* in a system in such a way that they are separated from one another, and from the protection controls of the operating system

ISSA Information Systems Security Association, non-profit society for security professionals. The organization has a Web site at *www.issa.org*, and has many local chapters.

ITIL Information Technology Infrastructure Library from the Office of Government Commerce (OGC) in the U.K. This is a set of guides and recommendations on the management of IT systems and services. As part of management, it has implications for the security of systems.

iterative simply means repeating or repeated. When used in respect of *software development*, refers to a method that allows for a return to a previous stage. From the perspective of security, non-iterative methods are preferred, since they force discipline in the process and design of software. Non-iterative methods include the waterfall, structured programming, cleanroom, and spiral. (Spiral is particularly useful for secure software development, since it imposes even more structure on the process, including an assessment step at each phase of the process.) Iterative development methods include such models as Joint Analysis Development (JAD), prototyping, Rapid Application Development (RAD), Modified Prototype Model (MPM), and exploratory.

J

Jerusalem one of the earliest MS-DOS *file infector viruses* known to be in the wild. Originally discovered and probably written in Israel. Originally known as the Israeli virus, it has also been called PLO, Friday the 13th, and 1813. Still one of the most widespread of file infecting viral programs and widely used as a template for the development of variant viral strains.

joke program see *prank*

journalling storage, or transfer to storage, of transactions, rather than the resultant data. The idea is that transactions are easier to reproduce than (say) an entire database, and the database can be reproduced, at need, by a batch processing of the journalled transactions.

K

Kerberos *single sign-on* system that uses *symmetric key encryption* via a *ticket-oriented* mechanism

key data used in cryptosystems to perform *encryption*. Sometimes called a *cryptovariable*.

key length since most modern *encryption* algorithms are mathematically based, the length of *keys* is a major determining element in the strength of an algorithm, or the work factor involved in breaking a cryptographic system. See also *key space*.

key management process of handling and controlling *cryptographic keys* and related material (such as intialization values) during their life cycle in a cryptographic system, including ordering, generating, distributing, storing, loading, escrowing, archiving, auditing, and destroying the material.

key pair in an *asymmetric encryption* system, a private, or confidential, *key* and its (mathematically) related public key. See also *private key* and *public key*.

key space range of possible values of a *cryptographic key*, or the number of distinct transformations supported by a particular cryptographic algorithm. Key space is actually a better determinant of cryptographic strength than simple *key length*.

keyed hash *cryptographic hash* or *digest* in which the mapping to a *hash result* is varied by a second input parameter that is a cryptographic *key*. If the input data object is changed, a new hash result cannot be correctly computed without knowledge of the secret key. Thus, the secret key protects the hash result so it can be used as a *checksum* even when there is a threat of an active attack on the data.

keylogger type of *keystroke monitor* as employed in *malware*

keystroke monitor device or system that records every key struck by a user. See also *key logger*.

KISS principle "Keep It Simple, Stupid," a maxim often invoked when discussing design to fend off creeping featurism and control development complexity. In regard to security, espousing the belief that simplicity is inherently more secure, as per C. A. R. Hoare, "There are two ways of constructing a software design: one way is to make it so simple that there are obviously no deficiencies, and the other way is to make it so complicated that there are no obvious deficiencies," and somewhat seconded by Niklaus Wirth, "Increasingly, people seem to misinterpret complexity as sophistication, which is baffling—the incomprehensible should cause suspicion rather than admiration."

kit refers to a program that produces a *virus* from a menu or a list of characteristics. Use of a virus kit involves no skill on the part of the author. Fortunately, most virus kits produce easily identifiable code. Packages of antiviral utilities are sometimes referred to as tool kits, occasionally leading to confusion of the terms.

knowledge base data structure consisting of a set of structures and a set of association descriptions that represents (possibly uncertain) knowledge about a given field. The relevance to security lies in the fact that decisions are often made based on the assumption that the knowledge is certain, a definite lack of integrity.

known-plaintext attack *cryptanalysis* technique in which the analyst tries to determine the *key* from knowledge of some *plaintext-ciphertext* pairs, although the analyst may also have other clues, such as knowing the *cryptographic algorithm*

L

label piece of information that represents the *security level* of an *object* and describes the sensitivity of the information in the object

labelling means to identify the sensitivity of a unit of information (*object*) or a process (*subject*), or, in a system supporting *mandatory access controls*, the assignment of sensitivity labels to every subject or object in the system

latency situation in which a system may be penetrated but some time may elapse between the penetration and further activity. This term is generally used in connection with *malware* such as *viruses* and *worms*. A virus with a long latent period may have time to reproduce and spread further before an overt *payload* renders detection likely. On the other hand, since viruses *in the wild* are regularly detected within hours of release, a latent period may simply ensure that the virus is eliminated before it has a chance to *trigger*.

latent flaw *vulnerability* unintentionally introduced during development, before it has been discovered by attackers, or the developer, researchers, or users. Although this term refers to the flaw itself, it is most commonly used in regard to discussions of *disclosure* in terms of the period between the release of a product for use, and the discovery of the vulnerability. See also *zero day*.

lattice model security model for information flow control in a system, based on the lattice that is formed by the security levels in a system and their partial ordering, possibly by subject or content. A simple example might be a grid with levels of security (management, internal, public) and different topic areas (customer data, research data, payroll). A manager in accounting would need to have management level access to payroll data, but would not necessarily need more than public access to research data.

Layer 2 Tunnelling Protocol (L2TP) Internet client-server protocol that combines aspects of PPTP (Point-to-Point Tunnelling Protocol) and L2F (Layer 2 Forwarding) and supports tunnelling of PPP (Point-to-Point Protocol) over an IP network or over frame relay or other switched network: it is a type of *virtual private network*. PPP can in turn encapsulate any OSI layer 3 protocol. Thus, L2TP does not specify security services; it depends on protocols layered above and below it to provide any needed security.

leapfrog attack use of information, access, or resources obtained illicitly from one host to compromise another host. Also, the act of connecting through one or more hosts to confuse a trace.

least privilege principle that requires that each *subject* be granted the most restrictive set of privileges needed for the performance of authorized tasks. The application of this principle limits the damage that can result from accident, error, or unauthorized use.

Lehigh one of the first MS-DOS *virus* programs, which only infected copies of the COMMAND.COM program. It is thought to have been isolated to the campus of Lehigh University where it was discovered, but most researchers and *vx* bulletin boards have copies. The limited use of bootable MS-DOS diskettes makes it unlikely that the virus would successfully spread if re-released.

letterbomb piece of email crafted to contain data that will be executed under certain conditions, usually related to the terminal or program used to display it, and intended to do nefarious things to the recipient's machine or terminal. Under UNIX, a letterbomb can try to get part of its contents interpreted as a shell command. See also *ANSI bomb* and *trojan horse*. Usage now somewhat archaic.

limited access synonymous with *access control*

limited disclosure form of *vulnerability disclosure* that holds that information about the vulnerability to the general public should be restricted in some manner, possibly being limited to announcements of the existence of the loophole, actions to be taken to restrict possible *exploits*, the existence of vendor *patches*, and so forth. Most often, restrictions are recommended in regard to the existence and distribution of exploit code. The term is not well defined or agreed to in general usage, and should be defined where used. Sometimes also restricted disclosure.

link the *virus* related term "link" is not used very widely and is used in a variety of ways. Amiga and Atari users talk about a link virus as a *file infector*. Some others use link to refer to a *system virus* or *cluster virus*.

link encryption application of online encryption or cryptographic operations to individual links of a communications system so that all information passing over the link is encrypted. See also *end-to-end encryption*.

list-oriented computer protection system in which each protected *object* has a list of all *subjects* authorized to access it. Compare *ticket-oriented*.

lock-and-key protection system protection system that involves matching a key or password with a specific access requirement

logic bomb resident computer program that triggers the perpetration of an unauthorized act when particular states of the system are realized or particular events occur. This may be a section of code, preprogrammed into a larger program, which waits for some trigger event to perform some damaging function. A *virus* may contain a logic bomb as a *payload*. Logic bombs that trigger on time events are sometimes known as time bombs, although this usage is not favored.

login act of a system entity gaining *access* to a session in which the entity can use system resources; usually accomplished by providing a username and password to an *access control* system that *authenticates* the user.

loophole error of omission or oversight in software or hardware that permits circumventing the system security policy. Compare *trap door* or *maintenance hook*.

Loveletter a script email *virus* that used Outlook and Windows Script Host. The virus spread itself as an email with an attachment called LOVE-LETTER-FOR-YOU.TXT.vbs. The filename was an interesting piece of social engineering, in that people were supposed to notice the .TXT and think the file was only a text file, and obviously were not supposed to notice the .vbs, the real extension that identifies the file as a script. Initially, the virus was widely referred to as the "Love Bug," but the more correct Loveletter or Love-Letter are now most common. Since Loveletter did not attach to other files, many call it a *worm*, but the virus did require user interaction, which a worm does not.

M

machine language computer language composed of machine instructions that can be executed directly by a computer without further modification

MacMag early Macintosh *virus* known also as Brandow, after the instigator (the publisher of the *MacMag* magazine), and Peace, after the message payload. MacMag has the dubious distinction of being the first virus known to have infected *commercial* software.

macro virus a macro is a small piece of programming in a simple language, used to perform a simple, repetitive function. Microsoft's Word Basic and VBA macro languages can include macros in data files, and have sufficient functionality to write complete *viruses*. Macro viruses therefore broke the long-held belief that viruses only infected executable files, and that data files were safe. *Script viruses* are similar in that they contain their own source code, although a macro virus is embedded in the data file, and a script virus is generally a standalone *object*.

magnetic remanence measure of the magnetic flux density remaining after removal of the applied magnetic force. Refers to any data remaining on magnetic storage media after removal of the power. Used both to assess the stability of magnetic media and to assess the likelihood of traces of data remaining after being deleted or *overwritten*.

mail storm condition in which many redundant messages are generated and sent, usually resulting from automated mail handling (such as vacation auto-responders replying to automatic forwarding mailing lists). Most modern mail systems have capabilities for dealing with common causes of mail storms.

mailbomb (n) excessively large volume of email (typically many thousands of messages) or one large message sent to a user's email account, for the purpose of crashing the system, or preventing genuine messages from being received
(v) to send a mailbomb

maintainability characteristic of design and installation that is expressed as the probability that an item will be retained in or restored to a specified condition within a given period of time

maintenance action taken to retain materiel, systems, or units in, or to restore to, a specified condition, including inspection, testing, servicing, classification as to serviceability, repair, rebuilding, reclamation, and sometimes additional feature development

maintenance hook special instructions in software to allow easy maintenance and additional feature development. These are not clearly defined during access for design specification. Hooks frequently allow entry into the code at unusual points or without the usual checks, so they are a serious security risk if they are not removed prior to live implementation. Maintenance hooks are special types of *backdoors* or *trap doors*.

malicious *virus* known to carry an intentionally damaging payload that will erase or corrupt files or data. It is felt by many antiviral researchers that all viral programs carry the potential for unintentional damage, since all viral programs change the target environment, and therefore the term "malicious virus" is assumed redundant. See *also benign.*

malicious logic hardware, software, or firmware that is intentionally included in a system for an unauthorized purpose; e.g., a *trojan horse* (military origin: limited usage, similarly for malicious code)

malware collective term including the many varieties of deliberately malicious software; that is, software written for the purpose of causing inconvenience, destruction, or the breaking of security policies or provisions. Malware is generally considered to include programs such as *DDoS* clients (or *zombies*), *logic bombs*, *RATs*, *trojan horses*, *viruses*, and *worms.* Malware is generally not considered to include unintentional problems in software, such as *bugs*, or deliberately written software that is not intended to do harm, such as *pranks*.

man-in-the-middle form of active wiretapping *attack* in which the attacker intercepts and selectively modifies communicated data to masquerade as one or more of the entities involved in a communication association. Similar to *hijacking*. For example, suppose Alice and Bob try to establish a session key by using the *Diffie-Hellman algorithm* without data origin authentication service. A "man in the middle" could (a) block direct communication between Alice and

Bob, then (b) *masquerade* as Alice sending data to Bob, (c) masquerade as Bob sending data to Alice, (d) establish separate session keys with each of them, and (e) function as a clandestine proxy server between them to capture or modify sensitive information that Alice and Bob think they are sending only to each other. Sometimes abbreviated MITM.

mandatory access control (MAC) means of restricting access to *objects* based on the sensitivity (as represented by a *label*) of the information contained in the objects and the formal authorization (i.e., clearance) of *subjects* to access information of such sensitivity. Compare *discretionary access control*.

marking process of placing a sensitivity designator or *label* with data such that its sensitivity is communicated. Marking is not restricted to the physical placement of a sensitivity designator, as might be done with a rubber stamp, but can involve the use of headers for network messages, special fields in databases, and so forth.

masquerading synonymous with *spoofing*

master boot record (MBR) on *ISA* or Wintel computers, the first physical (not logical) sector on the hard drive. The programming on this sector is called by the *BIOS* as part of the *boot* process, and the record also contains data about the structure of the hard drive in the partition table. See also *boot record*, *boot sector*, and *system boot record*.

maturity based on the Capability Maturity Model (CMM) originally developed at Carnegie-Mellon University, the concept of maturity is being applied to increasing numbers of enterprises and systems, including software, security, and business processes. Most of the resulting models use variations of the original five maturity levels, representing the experience and development of an institution. The levels are (1) initial (chaotic, immature), (2) repeatable (disciplined, capable), (3) defined (documented, consistent), (4) managed (predictable), and (5) optimising (constant improvement).

MBR see *master boot record*

media virus *virus* that catches the attention of the public, and particularly the media, generally out of proportion to its significance as a *threat*

meet in the middle specific form of *cryptanalytic attack* in which the attacker uses *known-plaintext* and the corresponding ciphertext to do both *encryption* and *decryption* to determine a multi-part *key*

Melissa type of Microsoft Word *macro virus* that also used functions in the Microsoft Outlook email program to spread itself very successfully and quickly. Technically, the Melissa code was not a macro, but a VBA (Visual Basic for Applications) script. Melissa is not considered a *script virus* since it was contained in a document.

meme expression first coined by Richard Dawkins (in the book *The Selfish Gene*, derived from the word *mimeme* to sound more like gene) for a unit of cultural transmission or imitation. The word *meme* has come to be used as a sort of standalone or quantum idea, and an idea considered as a replicator, particularly with the connotation that memes parasitize people into propagating them, much as viruses do. See *hoax* and *sig virus*.

meme virus see *hoax*

memory resident virus *virus* that stays in memory after it executes, and infects other files when certain conditions are met. In contrast, non-memory resident viruses, called *direct action*, are active only while an infected application runs.

message authentication code (MAC) data element associated with a message that allows a receiver to verify the integrity of the message

message digest see *digest*

metavirus see *hoax*

Michelangelo "descendent" of the Stoned boot sector/MBR *virus*, this program carries a damaging payload that triggers when the computer is booted on March 6th, the birth date of the Renaissance painter and sculptor. First discovered in early 1991, the virus gained notoriety during the "Michelangelo scare" leading up to March 1992. Although considered by many to have been media hype, the attention generated did disclose many thousands and possibly millions of infections prior to March 6th, which were disinfected and therefore never triggered. Michelangelo did survive 1992 and struck again in subsequent years, in some countries being the most widely reported virus as late as 1996.

microfortnight 1/1,000,000 of the basic unit of time in the Furlong/Firkin/Fortnight system of measurement, or 1.2096 second. (A furlong is 1/8th of a mile; a firkin is 1/4th of a barrel; the mass unit of the system is taken to be that of a firkin of water.)

Millennium Bug see *Y2K*

mimicking synonymous with *spoofing*

minimal protection (*TCSEC* Class D) class reserved for those systems that have been evaluated but fail to meet the requirements for a higher evaluation. Class D is frequently, and incorrectly, said to mean "no protection."

modes of operation description of the conditions under which a system functions, based on the sensitivity of data processed and the clearance levels and authorizations of the users. Four modes of operation are authorized (note that these modes originate with the U.S. government and military):
(1) Dedicated Mode—each user with direct or indirect individual access to the system, its peripherals, remote terminals, or remote hosts, has all of the following:
(a) A valid personnel clearance for all information on the system.
(b) Formal access approval for, and has signed nondisclosure agreements for all the information stored and/or processed (including all compartments, subcompartments, and/or special access programs).
(c) A valid need-to-know for all information contained within the system.

(2) System-High Mode—each user with direct or indirect access to the system, its peripherals, remote terminals, or remote hosts has all of the following:
(a) A valid personnel clearance for all information on the system.
(b) Formal access approval for, and has signed nondisclosure agreements for all the information stored and/or processed (including all compartments, subcompartments, and/or special access programs).
(c) A valid need-to-know for some of the information contained within the system.
(3) Compartmented Mode—each user with direct or indirect access to the system, its peripherals, remote terminals, or remote hosts, has all of the following:
(a) A valid personnel clearance for the most restricted information processed in the system.
(b) Formal access approval for, and has signed nondisclosure agreements for that information to which he/she is to have access.
(c) A valid need-to-know for that information to which he/she is to have access.
(4) Multilevel Mode—all the following statements are satisfied concerning the users with direct or indirect access to the system, its peripherals, remote terminals, or remote hosts:
(a) Some do not have a valid personnel clearance for all the information processed in the system.
(b) All have the proper clearance and the appropriate formal access approval for that information to which he/she is to have access.

(c) All have a valid need-to-know for that information to which they are to have access.

Moore's Law the logic density of silicon integrated circuits has closely followed a geometric curve; that is, the amount of information storable on a given amount of silicon, and the relative processing power, has roughly doubled every year, since the technology was invented. (The original prediction was made in 1965. In a much later interview, Gordon Moore admitted that he could not recall whether his original estimate was nine months, a year, eighteen months, or two years, but a pencil sketch made at the time seems to support a year.) This has implications for calculations of cryptographic work factor and the duration during which a given key length will be secure.

Morris Worm see *Internet Worm*

MtE most widely used abbreviation for the *polymorphic* or mutation engine written by the virus author known as *Dark Avenger*. Not a virus itself, this is a section of code that can be attached to any virus, giving the virus polymorphic features. Also known, less widely, as DAME (Dark Avenger's Mutation Engine).

MTX *multipartite virus* that reproduces by sending itself as an email message and by infecting program files. MTX will take control of the Internet connection of an infected machine, and seeks to bar access to many antiviral Web sites.

multilateral security as opposed to the usual multilevel security model (of information on different levels of security, such as top secret, secret, confidential, and public), multilateral security notes the differing needs for access based on the subject or content of the information. In military situations, for example, someone in a logistics and support position would need to know about overall troop movements, but would not need to know about strategy or tactics to be used.

multilevel device device that is used in a manner that permits it to simultaneously process data of two or more *security levels* without risk of compromise. To accomplish this, *sensitivity labels* are normally stored on the same physical medium and in the same form (i.e., machine-readable or human-readable) as the data being processed.

multilevel secure class of system containing information with different sensitivities that simultaneously permits access by users with different security clearances and needs-to-know, but prevents users from obtaining access to information for which they lack authorization

multilevel security mode see *modes of operation*

multipartite formerly a viral program that would infect both *boot sector*/MBRs and files. Now used to refer to a *virus* that will infect multiple types of *objects*, or reproduces in multiple ways.

multiple access rights terminal terminal that may be used by more than one class of users; for example, users with different access rights to data

multiuser mode of operation mode of operation designed for systems that process sensitive unclassified information in which users may not have a need-to-know for all information processed in the system. This mode is also for microcomputers processing sensitive unclassified information that cannot meet the requirements of the standalone mode of operation.

Murphy's Law commonly stated as "If anything can go wrong it will." This fatalistic sentiment is, in fact, a corruption of the original assertion, by engineer Edward A. Murphy, Jr. in 1949, that if you design a system or component that a technician (or user) can connect (or use) improperly, at some point he or she will. If the world can misunderstand your famous quote, it will.

mutating virus see *polymorphic*

mutual suspicion state that exists between interacting processes (subsystems or programs) in which neither process can expect the other process to function securely with respect to some property. Also describes the expected behaviour of individuals in any group of Famous Security Experts.

N

National Computer Security Center (NCSC) originally named the Department of Defense Computer
Security Center, the NCSC is responsible for
encouraging the widespread availability of trusted
computer systems throughout the U.S. Federal
Government

**National Security Decision Directive 145
(NSDD 145)** signed by U.S. President Reagan on
September 17, 1984, this directive is entitled
"National Policy on Telecommunications and
Automated Information Systems Security." It provides initial objectives, policies, and an organizational structure to guide the conduct of national
activities toward safeguarding systems that process,
store, or communicate sensitive information; establishes a mechanism for policy development; and
assigns implementation responsibilities.

**National Telecommunications and
Information Systems Security Advisory
Memoranda/Instructions (NTISSAM, NTISSI)**
NTISS Advisory Memoranda and Instructions provide advice, assistance, or information of general
interest on telecommunications and systems security
to all applicable U.S. federal departments and agencies. NTISSAMs/NTISSIs are promulgated by the
U.S. National Manager for Telecommunications and
Automated Information Systems Security and are
recommendations rather than legislation.

National Telecommunications and Information System Security Directives (NTISSD) NTISS Directives establish national-level decisions relating to NTISS policies, plans, programs, systems, or organizational delegations of authority. NTISSDs are promulgated by the Executive Agent of the Government for Telecommunications and Information Systems Security, or by the Chairman of the NTISSC when so delegated by the Executive Agent. NTISSDs are binding upon all federal departments and agencies. U.S. government and military.

need to know necessity for access to, knowledge of, or possession of specific information required to carry out official duties. Using a play on the phrases "need to know" and "need to know, now," a British mailing list, NTKnow, collects news items of interest to the stereotypical computer geek, but takes greatest delight in any instance of government, "official," or corporate actions detrimental to networking and computing, particularly in relation to security.

netiquette (network etiquette) conventions of polite behaviour recognized on Usenet and in mailing lists, such as avoidance of cross-posting to inappropriate groups, proper use of "out of office" automated replies, and refraining from commercial advertising

NAT network address translation means to allow a network to use one set of IP addresses (usually non-routable) for internal traffic and a second set of addresses for external traffic. The NAT server changes the source address, and usually also the port, of outgoing packets from the internal to the external address and reverses it for packets returning. NAT can be used to map a large number of computers onto a small assigned address space, but also hides the internal structure of the network from attackers and probes.

network forensics collection and analysis of evidence of intrusion or malfeasance from network activity and data. Closely related to *intrusion detection systems* and one of the major divisions of *digital forensics*.

network front end device that implements the necessary network protocols, including security-related protocols, to allow a computer system to be attached to a network

network weaving technique using different communication networks to gain access to a target system. Although the technique is widely known, this term is seldom used. It seems to relate primarily to the use of commercial networks.

newage unexamined and syncretistic beliefs, generally used in *social engineering* activity. The term derives from the messy melange of creeds known as the "New Age Movement." The term can be used as either an adjective or noun, and rhymes with "sewage."

Nimda based on the earlier *Code Red worm* or *virus*, and possibly programmed by the same author(s), Nimda corrected earlier errors and refined the targeting algorithms. It also extended the variety of ways it travelled and the type of *infection* mechanisms used, bringing *multipartite* technology to server worms.

Ninety-Ninety Rule "The first 90% of the code accounts for the first 90% of the development time. The remaining 10% of the code accounts for the other 90% of the development time." Attributed to Tom Cargill of Bell Labs.

no-lone zone room or other space to which no person may have unaccompanied *access* and that, when occupied, is required to be occupied by two or more appropriately authorized persons

No-OP (NOP) *opcode* that performs no operation. Also known as null-OP or NOP. Frequently used by *wannabe virus* writers (*vxers*) who will take an existing virus and modify it by sprinkling NOPs through the code until signature scanners no longer recognize it. Also sometimes used in *buffer overflows*: a string of NOPs creates a "No-OP sled" that provides a path to the code the attacker wants to execute.

noise disturbances superimposed upon a signal that tend to obscure its information content

nonce randomly generated value used to defeat replay attacks. The concepts of *challenge/response, initialization vector, nonce,* and *salt* are closely related. Challenge/response is generally used in regard to password and authentication schemes, initialization vector to block ciphers, nonce to short, automated network messages, and salt to password storage.

non-discretionary security possibly the original term for what is now known as *mandatory access control.* There may be a possible difference in that non-discretionary security explicitly requires both multi-level and multilateral security: restricting by clearance level and by topic.

non-inference model computer systems model that gives the impression to a user that he or she owns the entire resources of the machine. All responses to a user's request for resources are as if no other users are on the machine.

non-interference model computer systems model that prevents one user from interfering with or perturbing the resources or processing done by another. Most modern computer systems would follow this model to a greater or lesser extent.

nonrepudiation property of a system or service that provides protection against false denial of involvement in a communication. Although more properly written as "non-repudiation," the non-hyphenated version is more prevalent in actual usage.

NSDD 145 see *National Security Decision Directive 145*

nVIR early Macintosh *virus*, the source code for which was inadvertently published electronically. Shortly thereafter, two versions were found *in the wild*.

O

object passive entity that contains or receives information. *Access* to an object potentially implies access to the information it contains. Examples of objects are records, blocks, pages, segments, files, directories, directory trees, and programs, and bits, bytes, words, fields, processors, video displays, keyboards, clocks, printers, and network nodes.

object reuse reassignment and reuse of a storage medium (e.g., page frame, disk sector, magnetic tape) that once contained one or more *objects*. To be securely reused and assigned to a new *subject*, storage media must contain no residual data (*magnetic remanence*) from the object(s) previously contained in the media.

ohnosecond that minuscule fraction of time between hitting the "send" button and realizing that you have just posted your private *key* to alt.script-kiddies

on-access scanner real-time *virus scanner* that scans disks and files automatically and often in the background. An on-access scanner scans files for viruses as the computer accesses the files. Previously known as a resident scanner.

on-demand scanner *virus scanner* started manually by the user, or invoked under certain conditions or a regular schedule. Most on-demand scanners allow the user to set various configurations and to scan specific files, folders, or disks. Previously known as a manual scanner.

one-time pad *encryption* system based on a series of *keys*, each of which is used only once. Given certain limits on the length of the key in relation to the length of the message, and the use of a secure channel for transmission of the pad, one-time pads are considered unbreakable.

one-time password *authentication token* meant to be used for a single instance, and then discarded

one-way encryption irreversible transformation of *plaintext* to *ciphertext*, such that the plaintext cannot be recovered from the ciphertext by other than exhaustive procedures even if the cryptographic *key* is known. One-way encryption may seem odd, but it does have legitimate uses, such as storage of passwords.

onion routing technique for anonymizing routing, and therefore making *traffic analysis* and tracing more difficult. The packets transiting a chain of onion routers (from among the group in existence in the public network) have *encrypted* headers, and are passed from one to another before being sent to the eventual destination. Each router has the task of encrypting the socket connections and to act in turn as a proxy in the chain. The concept is similar to that used by the *cypherpunks* remailers for *anonymous* email communications.

opcode machine language instruction, usually consisting of a single byte, frequently with two or three bytes of argument following

open security environment environment that includes those systems in which at least one of the following conditions holds true: (1) Application developers (including maintainers) do not have sufficient clearance or authorization to provide an acceptable presumption that they have not introduced malicious logic. (2) Configuration control does not provide sufficient assurance that applications are protected against the introduction of malicious logic prior to and during the operation of system applications.

open source software development philosophy based on the premise that the source code for software must be made available to the user, and that restrictions cannot be made on the user's modification of the code, as long as the user is also bound by the same proviso. There are some disagreements about the precise use of open source, but it is generally seen as being akin but not equal to both *public domain* software and *freeware*. However, open source software is also seen as a viable *commercial* model. Compare with *shareware*.

operation restrictor similar to an activity monitor, an operation restrictor alerts the user to unusual or dangerous computer operations, and actually restricts them. Also known as activity blocker or behaviour blocker.

Operations Security (OPSEC) analytical process by which the U.S. government and its supporting contractors can deny to potential adversaries information about capabilities and intentions by identifying, controlling, and protecting evidence of the planning and execution of sensitive activities and operations.

Orange Book alternate name for the U.S. Department of Defense Trusted Computer Security Evaluation Criteria, because of the colour of the cover of the printed manual. The books in this series are collectively known as the *Rainbow Series* or the Rainbow Books because of the various colours used for covers.

out of band transfer of information using a channel that is outside or separate from the channel that is normally used. Out of band mechanisms are often used to distribute shared secrets (e.g., a *symmetric key*) or other sensitive information items that are needed to initialize or otherwise enable the operation of *cryptography* or other security mechanisms. In addition, the transfer of command information on the same channels as other data can lead to security problems, such as happened with older phone systems where trunk access and other controls were transmitted by tones within the voice band. See also *covert channel*.

output feedback (OFB) *block cipher* mode that modifies *electronic codebook* mode to operate on *plaintext* segments of variable length less than or equal to the block length. This mode operates by directly using the algorithm's previously generated output block as the algorithm's next input block (i.e., by "feeding back" the output block) and combining (*exclusive XOR-ing*) the output block with the next plaintext segment (of block length or less) to form the next *ciphertext* segment.

overt channel path within a computer system or network that is designed for the authorized transfer of data. Compare *covert channel*.

overwrite procedure process or stimulation to change the state of a bit or other data, which generally makes it impossible to recover original data without physically examining the media. Note that care must be taken to ensure that all slack, "unused," and system swap areas are overwritten, or residual data traces may be recovered. See also *format* and *magnetic remanence*.

owner individual or group that has responsibility for specific data, data types, or systems, and is charged with the communication of the need for certain security-related handling procedures to both the users and custodians of this data. Frequently now denoted as *data owner*.

P

packet in data communication, a sequence of binary digits, including data and control signals, that is transmitted and switched as a composite whole. The data, control signals, and possibly error control information are arranged in a specific format, according to the communications *protocol*. In the TCP/IP world, packets have specific names under different protocols and different layers. At the application layer, TCP (Transmission Control Protocol) has streams and UDP (User Datagram Protocol) messages. At the transport layer, TCP has segments and UDP packets. At the Internet (network) layer are datagrams, and at the network access (data link) layer are frames.

packet filter one of the simplest and earliest forms of a *firewall*, a packet filter accepts or rejects traffic based on source and destination addresses, and possibly the type of traffic

padding string of random data, typically added to *plaintext* in a block cipher when the last plaintext block is short, or the original data contains long strings of null data

pagejacking contraction of "Web page hijacking." A masquerade *attack* in which the attacker copies a home page or other material from the target server, rehosts the page on a server the attacker controls, and causes the rehosted page to be indexed by the major Web search services, thereby diverting browsers from the target server to the attacker's server. This practice is infrequent, and usage of this term is rare. This term should not be confused with other forms of Web diversion.

parity (1) error correcting code that will detect and possibly repair any single-bit error in the data block to which it is applied. See also *code, checksum, forward error correction*, and *redundancy*.

(2) state of equality or balance.

partitioned security mode mode of operation wherein all personnel have the clearance but not necessarily formal access approval and *need to know* for all information contained in the system. Not to be confused with compartmented security mode (see *modes of operation*).

passive *attack* that does not result in an unauthorized state change, such as an attack that only monitors and/or records data. See *active*.

password protected/private character string used to *authenticate* an identity

password attack attempt to obtain or decrypt a legitimate user's password. Attackers can use password dictionaries, cracking programs, and password sniffers in password attacks. Defence against password attacks is rather limited, but usually consists of a password policy including a minimum length, unrecognizable words, and frequent changes. See also *dictionary attack* and *password sniffing*.

password length equation equation that determines an appropriate *password* length, M, which provides an acceptable probability, P, that a password will be guessed in its lifetime. The password length is given by M = (log S)/(log N), where S is the size of the password space and N is the number of characters available. The password space is given by S = LR/P, where L is the maximum lifetime of a password and R is the number of guesses per unit of time. See also *password length parameter* and *key space*.

password length parameter basic parameter affecting the password length needed to provide a given degree of security. Password length parameters are related by the expression P = LR/S, where P is the probability that a password can be guessed in its lifetime, L is the maximum lifetime a password can be used to log in to a system, R is the number of guesses per unit of time, and S is the number of unique passwords (the password space). The degree of password security is determined by the probability that a password can be guessed in its lifetime.

password sniffing use of a network *sniffer* program to capture passwords as they cross a network. The network could be a local area network, or the Internet itself. The sniffer can be hardware or software. Most sniffers are passive and have sufficient intelligence to log only passwords.

password space total number of possible passwords that can be created by a given password generation scheme

patch quick modification of a program, which is sometimes a temporary fix until the problem can be solved in a more rigorous manner. A patch is generally a section of code that is overlaid on an existing program or system, similar to a patch on fabric.

Patches have two relations to security. A security *vulnerability* or *loophole* in a system may be fixed with a patch. However, because patches are not always subject to rigorous systems development procedures, they may also introduce vulnerabilities and loopholes into a system. Because of this, many enterprises are now instituting formal patch management procedures, similar to *change management*.

payload destructive or security-breaking activity, usually considered separately from its delivery mechanism, which may be a *trojan horse*, *virus*, or other means of transmission or emplacement. Payloads may be simple messages, or may be *logic bombs*, *trap doors*, or other functions. See also *malware*.

PC compatible see *ISA*

penetration successful act of bypassing the security mechanisms of a system

penetration signature characteristics or identifying marks that may be produced by a penetration. This signature may be used in *intrusion detection systems.*

penetration study study to determine the feasibility and methods for defeating controls of a system

penetration testing portion of security testing in which the evaluators attempt to circumvent the security features of a system. The evaluators may be assumed to use all system design and implementation documentation, which may include listings of system source code, manuals, and circuit diagrams. The evaluators work under the same constraints applied to ordinary users. Frequently abbreviated to pen test.

perfect forward secrecy see *forward secrecy*

perimeter-based security technique of securing a network or system by controlling *access* to all entry and exit points

periods processing processing of various levels of sensitive information at distinctly different times. Under periods processing, the system must be purged of all information from one processing period before transitioning to the next when there are different users with differing authorizations. See also *temporal isolation*.

permission description of the type of authorized interactions a *subject* can have with an *object*. Examples include read, write, execute, add, modify, and delete. Sometimes referred to as privilege or rights.

persistent storage any storage medium that remains intact when the power to it is disconnected. Also known as non-volatile storage.

personnel security procedures established to ensure that all personnel who have access to sensitive information have the required authority and appropriate clearances

PGP widely used and highly regarded *encryption* program using a hybrid *symmetric/ asymmetric* encryption system and a non-hierarchical *web of trust certificate* model. Many versions exist, including *commercial*, international, and *open source*. Not all versions are compatible in all functional areas.

phage another of the (many) idiosyncratic terms for *virus* or *malware*. Imprecise: should not be used.

pharming maliciously redirecting a Web browser to an alternate Web site (not the site the user is expecting) to fool the user into providing confidential data, which is then generally used for *identity theft* or other forms of fraud

phishing posting of a fraudulent message to a large number of people via *spam* or other general posting asking them to submit personal or security information, which is then used for further fraud or *identity theft*. The term is possibly an extension of trolling, which is the posting of an outrageous message or point of view (see *flame*) in a newsgroup or mailing list in the hope that someone will "bite" and respond to it.

phreak those who are interested in breaking into or otherwise manipulating the telephone system are referred to (and refer to themselves) as "phone phreaks," using the punning variant spelling. This is generally shortened to phreaks in common usage. The act of manipulating the phone system is known as phreaking.

physical control see *controls*

physical security application of physical barriers and control procedures as preventive measures or countermeasures against threats to resources and sensitive information

piggyback gaining unauthorized access to a system via another user's legitimate connection. See *between-the-lines entry* and *TOC/TOU.*

ping of death attack that sends an improperly large *ICMP* echo request packet (a "ping"), with the intent of overflowing the input buffers of the destination machine and causing it to crash

ping sweep attack that sends *ICMP* echo requests ("pings") to a range of IP addresses, with the goal of finding hosts that can be probed for *vulnerabilities*

PKI Public Key Infrastructure, a framework established to issue, maintain, and revoke public key certificates accommodating a variety of security technologies

plaintext original, or extracted, message, before the process of *encryption* or after the process of *decryption.* Generally also known as *cleartext.* However, technically, plaintext can be *ciphertext* that was the output of a prior stage in multiple stage encryption, whereas cleartext is always assumed to be intelligible to anyone.

pnambic (acronym from the scene in the film version of *The Wizard of Oz* in which the true nature of the wizard is first discovered: "Pay no attention to the man behind the curtain.") Of or pertaining to a process or function whose apparent operations are wholly or partially falsified. See also *security by obscurity.*

policy organizational-level rules governing acceptable use of computing resources, security practices, and guiding development of operational procedures.

Policies are supported by more detailed *guidelines, procedures,* and *standards.*

polymorphic pertaining to techniques that use some system of changing the form of a *virus* on each *infection* to try to avoid detection by *signature* scanning software. (The Greek roots literally mean "many forms.") Less sophisticated systems are referred to as self-encrypting.

port scan *attack* that sends client requests to a range of server port addresses on a host, with the goal of finding an active port and *exploiting* a known *vulnerability* of that service

prank software that appears to cause problems or damage, but in fact does not. In a sense, the inverse of the *trojan horse*. Books and programs are now being sold that perform these "stupid computer tricks." May cause heart problems, but no erasure of data. (It is, however, sometimes difficult to draw a hard and fast line between pranks and malware. Pranks generally cause some *denial of service*, but hopefully only for a short time.)

Preferred Products List (PPL) list of commercially produced equipment that meets *TEMPEST* and other requirements prescribed by the U.S. National Security Agency.

Pretty Good Privacy see *PGP*

preventative control see *controls*

preventive control see *controls*

preventive maintenance systematic and/or prescribed actions intended to reduce the probability of failure

print suppression eliminating the displaying of characters to preserve their secrecy; e.g., not displaying the characters of a password as it is keyed at the input terminal

privacy the concept of privacy is very difficult to nail down. Technically, it is often defined as the condition of being isolated from view, or secret. Those more concerned with social aspects generally speak of the ability to control information about oneself. Some definitions are:

(1) The right of an entity (normally a person), acting on its own behalf, to determine the degree to which it will interact with its environment, including the degree to which the entity is willing to share information about itself with others.

(2) The right of individuals to control or influence what information related to them may be collected and stored, and by whom, and to whom, that information may be disclosed.

You should not use this term as a synonym for *confidentiality*, which is a different concept. Privacy is a reason for security rather than a kind of security. For example, a system that stores personal data needs to protect the data to prevent harm, embarrassment, inconvenience, or unfairness to any person about whom data is maintained, and to protect the person's privacy. For that reason, the system may need to provide data confidentiality service. See also *anonymity*.

private key term often used to refer either to the shared *key* in a *symmetric encryption* system, or the confidential part of the *key pair* used in an *asymmetric* system

privilege see *permission*

privileged instructions set of instructions (e.g., interrupt handling or special computer instructions) to control features (such as storage protection features) that are generally executable only when the automated system is operating in the executive state

probe device or program used to gather information about a system or its users

procedural security synonymous with *administrative security*

procedure part of the supporting structure of a security *policy*, a procedure is a set of steps and instructions to be specifically followed under certain conditions

process program in execution. See *domain* and *subject*.

promiscuous mode state where a network interface can capture all network traffic irrespective of the *packet* destination address. Promiscuous mode is required for many network *attacks*, but also for various network utilities.

proprietary refers to information (or other property) that is owned by an individual or organization and for which the use is restricted by that entity

protection–critical portions of the TCB those portions of the *TCB* whose normal function is to deal with the control of *access* between *subjects* and *objects*.

Their correct operation is essential to the protection of the data on the system.

protection philosophy informal description of the overall design of a system that delineates each of the protection mechanisms employed. A combination, appropriate to the evaluation class, of formal and informal techniques is used to show that the mechanisms are adequate to enforce the security policy.

protection ring one of a hierarchy of privileged modes of a system that gives certain *access* rights to *user* programs and processes authorized to operate in a given mode. This term is now commonly applied to operating modes of the Intel Pentium processor, and the Windows NT and 2000 operating systems, although the later usage may not be fully consistent with earlier definitions.

protocol set of rules and formats, semantic and syntactic, that permits entities to exchange information

proxy server computer attached to two or more networks, providing service to more than one client or server as if to a single machine. Most often used to connect multiple machines on a local area network to a public network such as the Internet. Often used as a type of *firewall*, since the proxy server can be hardened, and *attacks* will be directed against the proxy server rather than the actual servers behind it. See *also application level gateway* and compare with *packet filter*.

pseudo flaw apparent loophole deliberately implanted in an operating system program as a trap for intruders. See also *honeypot* and *entrapment*.

pseudorandom the generation of random numbers is very important to operations related to *cryptography*. As Robert R. Coveyou has said, "[t]he generation of random numbers is too important to be left to chance." If, for example, *keys* are not chosen at random, then key choice may be determinable, and thus the cryptographic system may be compromised. However, it is not possible to produce truly random numbers with a program. The great John Louis von Neumann himself stated, "[a]nyone who considers arithmetical methods of producing random numbers is, of course, in a state of sin." (The Dilbert cartoon strip made a profound observation on October 25, 2001 when, in response to a random number generator that produced only nines, Dilbert asked if it was truly random, and was told "That's the problem with randomness. You can never be sure.") Therefore, extensive efforts are put into creating functions that randomize input, and include event data (such as system clock times, time sequences between keystrokes, and even electronic noise) as input to obtain data that is as random as possible for use in cryptographic systems.

public domain legal term that carries the same meaning in regard to software that it does in the field of literature. Software in the public domain may be used by anyone, for any purpose, in any manner, without restriction. This term is often used carelessly to refer to *freeware*, which requires no payment, but for which the author still assumes copyright and control, and *shareware*, which does, in fact, require payment for continued use. See also *commercial* and *open source*.

public key sometimes used to refer generically to *asymmetric encryption* systems, but more properly referring to the non-confidential portion of a *key pair* in asymmetric systems

public key forward secrecy see *forward secrecy*

Public Law 100-235 (P.L. 100-235) also known as the Computer Security Act of 1987, this U.S. law created minimum acceptable security practices for improving the security and privacy of sensitive information in federal computer systems. This law assigned to the National Institute of Standards and Technology (NIST) responsibility for developing standards and guidelines for federal computer systems processing unclassified data. The law also required establishment of security plans by all operators of federal computer systems that contained sensitive information.

purge removal of sensitive data from a system, system storage device, or peripheral device with storage capacity, at the end of a processing period. This action is performed in such a way that there is *assurance* proportional to the *sensitivity* of the data that the data may not be reconstructed. A system must be disconnected from any external network before a purge. After a purge, the medium can be *declassified* by observing the review procedures of the respective agency.

Q

quantum encryption system has been developed using polarized photons to communicate over fibre optic cable. This may be used for negotiation of a *session key* since an adversary listening in on the line can obtain only half of the required information. This should not be confused with the conjectural use of computer circuits that may be able to calculate all possible solutions to a problem simultaneously to find the correct one, thus being hypothetically able to perform *brute force* attacks of arbitrary size.

R

rabbit *virus* that generates multiple copies of itself without attaching to other programs. Generally, this type of *attack* is a *denial of service* based on excessive use of disk or memory space or CPU cycles. Usage rare. See *wabbit*.

RADIUS see *Remote Authentication Dial-In User Service*

Rainbow Series set of more than 30 technical and policy publications issued by the National Computer Security Center (NCSC) and informally named for the colours of the covers. The *Orange Book (TCSEC)* is possibly the best known of the series.

random in mathematics, random means unpredictable. A sequence of values is called random if each successive value is obtained merely by chance and does not depend on the preceding values of the sequence, and a selected individual value is called random if each of the values in the total population of possibilities has equal probability of being selected. In *cryptography* and other security applications, random means unpredictable, and unguessable. When selecting data values to use for cryptographic *keys*, the requirement is for data that an adversary has a very low probability of guessing or determining. See *pseudorandom*.

RAT (Remote Access Trojan) program designed to provide access to, and control over, a network-attached computer from a remote computer or location, in effect providing a *backdoor*. Interestingly, RATs are often described by their creators as "Remote

Administration Tools" in an attempt to present them as legitimate utility software. The distinction between valid remote tools and RATs generally lies in the provisions for RATs to be installed without the direct knowledge of the user or operator of the computer to be controlled, and additional functions to announce the installation of the RAT, and the address of the computer being controlled, to public venues such as Usenet newsgroups and IRC (Internet Relay Chat).

read fundamental operation that results only in the flow of information from an *object* to a *subject*

read access *permission* to read information

real time pertaining to the performance of a computation during the actual time the related event occurs, so results of the computation can be used in guiding the physical process, or transactions can be processed and the data immediately available, rather than being batched for later processing. Real–time processing has particular security concerns since control systems frequently reduce operating system controls to improve performance, and database sharing and locking controls have their own security issues.

real-time scanner see *on-access scanner*

recertification ongoing reassurance that a previously certified unclassified computer application processing sensitive information has been periodically reviewed, that compliance with established protection policies and procedures remains in effect, and that security risks remain at an acceptable level

reconciliation in auditing, the identification and analysis of differences between values contained in two substantially similar files or between a detail file and a control total

recovery control see *controls*

recovery procedures actions necessary to restore a system's computational capability and data files after a system failure. See also *business continuity plan* and *disaster recovery plan.*

recursion see *recursion*. Recursion is a situation in which a process calls itself, possibly with modified parameters. Recursion does have a place in discussions of applications security, since improperly bounded or handled recursion can exhaust memory or create other problems for the program in operation.

redundancy duplication of system components (such as hard drives, power sources, or processors), information (such as *backup* copies of software or archived files), data symbols (such as *parity* or *Hamming code*), or personnel intended to increase the *reliability* or *availability* of service and/or decrease the risk of information loss

reference monitor *access control* concept that refers to an abstract machine that mediates all accesses to *objects* by *subjects*

reference validation mechanism implementation of the *reference monitor* concept. A *security kernel* is a type of reference validation mechanism.

Registry see *Windows Registry*

reliability probability of a given system performing its mission adequately for a specified period of time under the expected operating conditions. Reliability is generally considered as *availability* with the addition of the expectation of proper outcomes from processing: a sort of cumulative availability.

remap to make a software or configuration data modification that redirects system associations. The extent of remapping can vary widely. *ANSI bombs* can be used to remap the keyboard to invoke a *payload* command with a single keystroke. Other remapping may involve changes to network routing tables that may redirect the user from a trusted site to an unknown site. In a sense, the classic *man-in-the-middle attack* is a form of remapping.

remediation deliberate precautionary measures undertaken to improve the *reliability, availability*, and survivability of critical assets and/or infrastructures, particularly with regard to specific known *vulnerabilities* and *threats*. Remediation is a part of *risk management* and is closely allied to the concept of a *safeguard* or *countermeasure*.

Remote Access Trojan see *RAT*

Remote Authentication Dial-In User Service (RADIUS) Internet protocol (RFC 2138) for carrying dial-in users' *authentication* information and configuration information between a shared, centralized authentication server (the RADIUS server) and a network access server (the RADIUS client) that needs to authenticate the users of its network access ports. A user of the RADIUS client presents authentication information to the client, and the client passes that information to the RADIUS server. The server authenticates the client using a shared secret value, then checks the user's authentication information, and finally returns to the client all authorization and configuration information needed by the client to deliver service to the user.

replay attack *attack* in which a valid data transmission is maliciously or fraudulently repeated, either by the originator or by an adversary who intercepts the data and retransmits it, possibly as part of a masquerade attack

replicate in general, copying or reproduction. In *virus* research, the term "replicate," or sometimes "reproduction," is often used to distinguish the clandestine copying action done by a virus from the normal and deliberate duplication performed by the user.

repudiation denial by a system entity that was involved in an association (especially an association that transfers information) of having participated in the relationship. See *accountability* and *nonrepudiation*.

resident program that stays in the memory of the computer while other programs are running, waiting for a specific *trigger* event. Accessory software is often of this type, as is *activity monitoring* and resident or on-access *virus scanning* software. Viral programs often attempt to "go resident," and so this is one of the functions an activity monitor may check. Also known as "memory resident" and, in MS-DOS circles, TSR (Terminate and Stay Resident). The Microsoft Windows equivalent is a VxD or service, while the Novell NetWare version is NLM (Netware Loadable Module). UNIX resident programs are generally known as daemons, although there is a tendency to restrict this usage to network server software.

residual risk portion of risk that remains after security measures have been applied. The risk of a given *vulnerability* after the application of specific *safeguards*.

residue data left in storage after processing operations are complete, but before *degaussing* or rewriting has taken place

resilience ability of a system to withstand the impact of a failure or interruption

resource encapsulation process of ensuring that a resource not be directly accessible by a *subject*, but that it be protected so the *reference monitor* can properly mediate accesses to it.

restricted area any area to which access is subject to special restrictions or controls for reasons of security

retrovirus this term has been used to describe a *virus* that attempts to ensure that all *backup* copies of software are *infected* (presumably before setting off some kind of *payload*), or attempts to disable *antivirus* software. Neither meaning is accepted as a standard within virus research, and this term is not used within the research community.

reverse engineer to determine the internal workings of a system from externally available indications of function

RFC Request For Comments. In business and government, an RFC is just that. On the Internet, a proposal for a new protocol, usually made as a request for comments on the proposal, was frequently accepted as a useful tool if nobody had a better idea. Therefore, the term came to be used for the standards of the Internet. Most documents and standards are published as RFCs; there are also editorial and background papers, and even a few jokes.

risk expectation of loss expressed as the probability that a particular *threat* will *exploit* a particular *vulnerability* with a particular harmful result

risk acceptance decision to participate in an activity where a risk is known, but acceptable on the basis of the potential benefit of the activity

risk analysis also known as risk assessment, a process that systematically identifies valuable system resources and *threats* to those resources, quantifies loss exposures (i.e., loss potential) based on estimated frequencies and costs of occurrence, and (optionally) recommends how to allocate resources to countermeasures to minimize total exposure. The analysis lists risks in order of cost and criticality, thereby determining where countermeasures should be applied first. It is usually financially and technically infeasible to counteract all aspects of risk, so some *residual risk* will remain, even after all available countermeasures have been deployed.

risk avoidance decision not to participate in an activity where the potential benefit is perceived to be unacceptable due to a known risk

risk management process of identifying, controlling, and eliminating or minimizing uncertain events that may affect system resources

risk transference attempt to transfer risk or uncertainty to another party. Insurance is a form of risk transference.

robust ability to recover gracefully from a whole range of inputs and situations in a given environment. See also *exception*.

rogue program that breaks or escapes bounds in a partitioned computer, more generically used to describe any type of malicious or buggy software: a program that, because of a *bug* in programming, interferes with normal system operation. The damage caused by a rogue is unintentional. Used primarily in mainframe circles and now relatively rare.

ROM read only memory. A static memory type used to hold programming, regardless of power conditions. Primarily used for the "boot strap" programming for microcomputers. Until recently, this memory has been non-writable in normal operation, and so, safe from *virus* and other *attacks*, but this may change with the recent promotion and use of "flash" EEPROMs.

root authority *certification authority* (CA) at the top of a CA hierarchy

root kit script, set of scripts, or package of modified system programs used for gaining or keeping unauthorized root privileges (or equivalent supervisory powers) on a compromised system. Recently, media usage has expanded this definition to include any software that can hide software or processes on a system, but this usage is vague and should be avoided. Also rootkit.

rot13 from "rotate alphabet 13 places," simple Caesar-cypher *encryption* that replaces each English letter with the one 13 places forward or back along the alphabet

RSA *asymmetric cryptographic* algorithm named for its 1977 inventors—Ron Rivest, Adi Shamir, and Leonard Adleman. RSA uses exponentiation modulo the product of two large prime numbers. The difficulty of breaking RSA is believed to be equivalent to the difficulty of factoring integers that are the product of two large prime numbers of approximately equal size.

S

safeguard any protective measure or control that is prescribed to meet the security requirements specified
for a system. Safeguards may include but are not
necessarily limited to hardware and software security
features, operating procedures, *accountability* procedures, *access* and distribution controls, management
constraints, *personnel security*, and physical structures,
areas, and devices. Also sometimes specifically called
security safeguards. See also *countermeasure* and
control.

salami a story of a program that takes advantage of very
active systems to make incremental changes. The
usual tale is of a banking system that siphons frac-
tions of a penny at a time into the programmer's
account. In spite of the lack of evidence for the
existence of *attacks* of this type, increasing numbers
of security books make reference to it.

salt random data added to small amounts of information,
such as *passwords* or *session keys*, prior to *encryption* to
make *dictionary attacks* (a type of *brute force* attack)
more difficult or time consuming. When used, salt is
generally placed in front of the encrypted data. The
concepts of *challenge/response, initialization vector,
nonce,* and *seed* are closely related.
Challenge/response is generally used in regard to
password and authentication schemes, initialization
vector to block ciphers, nonce to short, automated
network messages, and salt to password storage. Salt
is also what you should take any guarantee of perfect security with a large grain of.

samurai *hacker* (technically astute individual) who hires out for legal cracking jobs, *penetration tests*, or semi-legal corporate intelligence. Usage limited and obscure. See also *dark-side hacker* and *whitehat*.

sandbox security model providing that code or programs from untrusted sources can be run in an environment that restricts potentially dangerous activities and functions. Originally arising from and applied to the Java language applet system, it may now refer also to the general concept.

sanitize to delete sensitive data from a file, a device, or a system; or modify data to be able to downgrade its *classification* level

sanity check programming whereby the application automatically checks input data for "reasonableness." For example, entry of non-numeric data in a numeric field should raise an error to be dealt with. Sanity checking is a type of *exception* handling.

sarchasm gulf of understanding, between speaker and hearer, so vast that the listener does not even realize the speaker is making fun of him/her. Sarchasm frequently backfires on security professionals: users are quite willing to assume that "Well, let's just eliminate passwords altogether, if those are too hard to remember!" is a really good idea, rather than an insult (based on suggestion by SW).

scan string see *signature*

scanner (1) program that reads the contents of a file looking for code known to exist in specific *virus* programs. Also referred to as known virus scanning (KVS).

(2) program that examines computers and network systems, examining configurations and looking for security *vulnerabilities*. This type of program can be used by both defenders and attackers. SATAN (Security Administrators Tool for Analysing Networks) is an example of this type of scanner.

scavenging searching through object *residue* to acquire unauthorized data

Scores Macintosh *virus* that seems to have been written with intent to cause problems for a specific company and software program. Because one of the most widely published reports of infection was from an office at NASA, it has also been referred to by that name.

scratch monkey a mythic story in computerdom, based on a true event involving the death of a monkey (Mabel, a research subject at the University of Toronto) due to troubleshooting and reconfiguration that interfered with specialized hardware. The exhortation to "always mount a scratch monkey" is a reminder never to do testing or development on a live system or data.

screened subnet isolated subnet created behind a *screening router* to protect the private network. The degree to which the subnet may be accessed depends on the screening rules in the router.

screening router router configured to permit or deny traffic using filtering techniques based on a set of permission rules installed by the administrator. A component of many *firewalls* usually used to block traffic between the network and specific hosts on an IP port level. Generally considered the lowest form of a firewall, it is used when speed or network performance is the major decision criteria.

script virus it is difficult to make a strong distinction between script and macro programming languages, but generally, a script *virus* is a standalone *object*, contained in a text file or email message. A *macro virus* is generally contained in a data file, such as a Microsoft Word document.

sector predetermined, addressable angular part of a track or a band on a magnetic drum or magnetic disk. Because the data laid down in a sector is a function of the speed and timing of the rotation speed, and because a margin is allowed for variation in that speed, a second form of *slack space* may be available, within that margin space, for those able to access and control the physical attributes of the hard disk.

sector virus see *cluster virus*

secure configuration management set of procedures appropriate for controlling changes to a system's hardware and software structure for the purpose of ensuring that changes will not lead to violations of the system's *security policy*

Secure Sockets Layer (SSL) Internet protocol (originally developed by Netscape Communications, Inc.) that uses connection-oriented end-to-end *encryption* to provide data *confidentiality* service and data *integrity* service for traffic between a client and a server, and that can optionally provide peer entity *authentication* between the client and the server. SSL is layered below HTTP and above a reliable transport protocol (TCP). SSL is independent of the application it encapsulates, and any higher level protocol can layer on top of SSL transparently. SSL has two layers: (a) SSL's lower layer, the SSL Record Protocol, is layered on top of the transport protocol and encapsulates higher level protocols. (b) SSL's upper layer provides *asymmetric cryptography* for server authentication (verifying the server's identity to the client) and optional client authentication (verifying the client's identity to the server), and also enables them to negotiate a *symmetric encryption* algorithm and secret *session key* (to use for data confidentiality) before the application protocol transmits or receives data. A *keyed hash* provides data integrity service for encapsulated data.

secure state as originally defined in the formal models that dealt only with *confidentiality*, a condition in which no *subject* can access any *object* in an unauthorized manner. Modern models may also include *integrity* and *availability*.

secure subsystem subsystem that contains its own implementation of the *reference monitor* concept for those resources it controls. However, the secure subsystem must depend on other controls and the base operating system for the control of *subjects* and the more primitive system *objects*.

security architecture plan and set of principles that describe (a) the security services a system is required to provide to meet the needs of its users, (b) the system elements required to implement the services, and (c) the performance levels required in the elements to deal with the *threat* environment. A complete system security architecture includes administrative security, communication security, computer security, emanations security, personnel security, and physical security. A complete security architecture needs to deal with both intentional, intelligent threats and accidental kinds of threats. See also *security policy*.

security association (1) a relationship established between two or more entities to enable them to protect data they exchange. The relationship is used to negotiate characteristics of protection mechanisms, but does not include the mechanisms themselves.
(2) in *IPsec* usage, a simplex (uni-directional) logical connection created for security purposes and implemented with either AH or ESP (but not both). The security services offered by a security association depend on the protocol selected, the IPsec mode (transport or tunnel), the endpoints, and the election of optional services within the protocol. A security association is identified by a (data) "triple" consisting of (a) a destination IP address, (b) a protocol (AH or ESP) identifier, and (c) a Security Parameter Index.

security audit independent review and examination of a system's *policy*, records, and activities to determine the adequacy of system controls, ensure compliance with established *security policy* and *procedures*, detect breaches in security services, and recommend any changes that are indicated for *countermeasures*. The basic audit objective is to establish *accountability* for system entities that initiate or participate in security-relevant events and actions. Thus, means are needed to generate and record security audit information and to review and analyze the *audit trail* to discover and investigate *attacks* and security *compromises.*

security by obscurity term used, usually pejoratively, to refer to the practice of attempting to secure a system by failing to publish information about it, in the hope that nobody will be able to figure out how it works

security cost benefit analysis detailed study of security measures, their technical and operational feasibility, and their associated costs and benefits

security critical mechanisms those security mechanisms whose correct operation is necessary to ensure the *security policy* is enforced

security domain set of *objects* a *subject* has the ability to *access*

security evaluation evaluation done to assess the degree of trust or *assurance* that can be placed in systems for the secure handling of sensitive information. One type, a product evaluation, is performed on the hardware and software features and assurances of a computer product from a perspective that excludes the application environment. The other type, a system evaluation, is done for the purpose of assessing a system's security *safeguards* with respect to a specific operational mission and is a major step in the *certification* and *accreditation* process.

security fault analysis security analysis, usually performed on hardware at gate level, to determine the security properties of a device when a hardware fault is encountered

security features security-relevant functions, mechanisms, and characteristics of system hardware and software. Security features are a subset of system security *safeguards*.

security filter trusted subsystem that enforces a *security policy* on the data that passes through it

security flaw error of commission or omission in a system that may allow protection mechanisms or *safeguards* to be bypassed. See also *loophole*.

security flow analysis security analysis performed on a formal system specification that locates potential flows of information within the system

security kernel hardware, firmware, and software elements of a *TCB* that implement the *reference monitor* concept. It must mediate all *accesses*, be protected from modification, and be verifiable as correct.

security label piece of information that represents the *security level* of an *object*

security level combination of a hierarchical *classification* and a set of nonhierarchical categories that represents the *sensitivity* of information

security measures elements of software, firmware, hardware, or procedures that are included in a system for the satisfaction of security specifications or *security policy*

security perimeter boundary where security controls are in effect to protect *assets*

security policy set of laws, rules, and practices that regulate how an organization manages, protects, and distributes sensitive information

security policy model formal presentation of the *security policy* enforced by the system. It must identify the set of rules and practices that regulate how a system manages, protects, and distributes sensitive information. See *Bell-La Padula* model and *formal security policy model.*

security range highest and lowest *security levels* that are permitted in or on a system, system component, subsystem, or network

security requirements types and levels of protection necessary for equipment, data, information, applications, and facilities to meet *security policy*

security requirements baseline description of minimum requirements necessary for a system to maintain an acceptable level of security

security review periodic assessment of the effectiveness and need for various *controls.* A security review may be conducted by the entity responsible for security provision, whereas a *security audit* should always be conducted by a separate entity.

security safeguards see *safeguard*

security specifications detailed description of the *safeguards* required to protect a system

security test and evaluation examination and analysis of the security *safeguards* of a system as they have been applied in an operational environment to determine the security posture of the system

security testing process used to determine that the *security features* of a system are implemented as designed. This includes hands-on functional testing, *penetration testing*, and *verification*.

seed value, which should be chosen as randomly as possible, used to start the process of generating *pseudorandom* numbers for *cryptographic* processes. See also related terms *nonce* and *salt*.

self-extracting file file that contains software to decompress part of itself into one or more parts when executed. Software authors and distributors often use this file type to transmit files and software via the Internet since the compressed files conserve disk space, reduce download time, and do not require the end user to obtain decompression programs. Although popular with neophyte Internet users because it does not require separate de-archiving programs, it presents a number of potential security *vulnerabilities*. Since compression provides a form of *encryption*, self-extracting files may hide *viruses* and other *malware*. In addition, many self-extracting formats contain functions to execute files immediately after extraction.

self-garbling virus see *polymorphic*

sensitive information any information that the loss, misuse, modification of, or unauthorized access to could affect the specific interest of the enterprise. U.S. government and military entities have specific regulations in this regard.

sensitivity label piece of information that represents the *security level* of an *object*. Sensitivity labels are used by the *TCB* as the basis for *mandatory access control* decisions.

separation of duties practice of dividing the steps in a system function among different individuals, to keep a single individual from subverting the process. In particular, a person doing *audit* or check functions should not be the person performing the operation. Originally part of the Clark-Wilson integrity model, where it refers to processes, rather than people.

session key key used for *symmetric encryption* to protect a single instance or session of communication. The key may be calculated or negotiated (the *Diffie-Hellman* system is an example), or it may be generated *randomly* or *pseudorandomly*, exchanged *out of band* or protected by *asymmetric* encryption (or a long-term shared symmetric key), and then discarded. The reason for the use of a session key, in the case of a pre-existing shared symmetric key, is that frequent use of symmetric keys gives away information about the key. See also *ephemeral key*, *forward secrecy*, *man-in-the-middle*, *quantum encryption*, and *salt*.

shareware software that is distributed widely, usually made available on anonymous download servers and Web sites. Users are encouraged to "try before you buy," but users who continue to use the software are supposed to pay for the programs. The honour system of distribution reduces overhead costs, and shareware is generally cheaper than *commercial* software. See also *freeware*, *open source*, and *public domain*.

shell scrap object Microsoft file format, one of the many that may include executable content. The shell scrap file extensions, .SHS and .SHB, will not display in normal Windows file dialogue boxes and the Windows Explorer unless a change is made to the Registry.

shrink wrap plastic film used to protect the packaging of *commercial* software. "Shrink wrapped software" is often used as a synonym for commercial software. Many people feel shrink wrap is some kind of protection, guarantee, or warranty. It isn't, since anyone with a roll of film, a hot wire, and a blow dryer can "shrink wrap" a package.

sig virus parasitic *meme* embedded in a signature block in email messages or postings. There was a meme plague or fad for these on Usenet in late 1991. Most were along the lines of "I am a sig virus, please reproduce me in your sig block." The sig virus' memetic hook is the amusement value of going along with the gag.

signature distinctive pattern used to detect a *virus infection* or system penetration (see *intrusion detection system*). In virus detection, the signature may be a fixed string of bytes, known as a scan string, although intricate signatures may be *algorithmically* based. System penetration signatures are generally more complex, and may involve comparison of data from a number of forms of *audit* and logging. See *scanner*.

simple integrity property the Biba integrity model essentially inverts the *Bell-La Padula* confidentiality model, and therefore the simple integrity property inverts the *simple security property* and states that, to preserve integrity, a *subject* cannot read from an *object* of lesser integrity

simple security condition see *simple security property*

simple security property *Bell-La Padula* security model rule allowing a *subject read access* to an *object* only if the *security level* of the subject *dominates* the security level of the object. In other words, you can read a file if your level is equal to or higher than that of the file. Synonymous with simple security condition.

single-level device device that is used to process data of only a single *security level* at any one time

single point of failure necessary resource or operation for which no *redundancy* exists, or which multiple redundant resources rely on for operation. Negligence in eliminating single points of failure is astoundingly common in disasters.

single sign-on system or procedure whereby a *user* is *authenticated* once, and thereafter has *access* to a number of disparate systems

Sisyphus the Perplexed patron saint of information security. See also *Eris*. Per AJA.

slack space generally, space allocated to a disk file, but not actually used to store information. Also note that data laid down in a *sector* is a function of the speed and timing of the rotation speed, and because a margin is allowed for variation in that speed, a second form of slack space may be available, within that margin space, for those able to access and control the physical attributes of the hard disk. Slack space can be used either in searching for locations from which evidence can be extracted in *computer forensics*, or to find hiding places for writing sections of *malware*.

smurfing *denial of service attack exploiting* IP broadcast addressing and *ICMP* ping *packets* to cause flooding. A smurf program builds a network packet that appears to originate from another address, that of the "victim," either a host or an IP router. The packet contains an ICMP ping message that is addressed to an IP broadcast address, to all IP addresses in a given network. The echo responses to the ping message return to the victim's address. The goal of smurfing may be to deny service at a particular host or to flood all or part of an IP network. A related attack, called fraggle, performs the same activity using UDP (User Datagram Protocol) packets.

sniffer program that monitors network traffic. Attackers use sniffers to capture data transmitted via a network. See *password sniffing*.

social engineering attacking or penetrating a system by tricking or subverting operators or users, rather than by means of a *technical attack*. More generally, the use of fraud, spoofing, or other social or psychological measures to get legitimate users to break *security policy*.

SOCKS Internet protocol (RFC 1928) that provides a generalized *proxy server* that enables client-server applications—such as telnet, ftp, and HTTP; running over either TCP or UDP—to use the services of a *firewall*. SOCKS is layered under the application layer and above the transport layer. When a client inside a firewall wishes to establish a connection to an *object* that is reachable only through the firewall, it uses TCP to connect to the SOCKS server, negotiates with the server for the *authentication* method to be used, authenticates with the chosen method, and then sends a relay request. The SOCKS server evaluates the request, typically based on source and destination addresses, and either establishes the appropriate connection or denies it.

Software Development Methodologies methodologies for specifying and verifying design programs for system development. See also *iterative*.

software security general-purpose (executive, utility, or software development) tools and applications programs or routines that protect data handled by a system

software system test and evaluation process process that plans, develops, and documents the quantitative demonstration of the fulfillment of all baseline functional performance, operational, and interface requirements

spam (1) (v) to indiscriminately send unsolicited, unwanted, irrelevant, or inappropriate messages, especially commercial advertising, in mass quantities. In sufficient volume, spam can cause *denial of service*. (2) (n) electronic "junk mail"

Yes, the term "spam," used in reference to masses of unwanted email or newsgroup postings, does derive from SPAM the canned meat. There is an opinion that says the term was used because spam pretends to be information in the same way SPAM pretends to be ... well, Hormel is a good sport about the neologistic appropriation of its trade name, so we won't belabor the point, beyond noting that the same speculation also makes an analogy between nonsense-content and fat-content. Hormel says, "We do not object to use of this slang term [spam] to describe [unsolicited commercial email (UCE)], although we do object to the use of our product image in association with that term. Also, if the term is to be used, it should be used in all lowercase letters to distinguish it from our trademark SPAM, which should be used with all uppercase letters." The more commonly accepted derivation is that the term comes from a comedy sketch, by the British group Monty Python, involving a restaurant where the menu items contain increasing amounts of SPAM, and the Viking clientele eventually drown out all dialogue by singing about "SPAM, SPAM, SPAM, SPAM, SPAM, SPAM, SPAM, SPAM" in a kind of conversational denial of service. Hormel themselves note this in a page at *www.spam.com/ci/ci_in.htm*.

(And where did Monty Python get the idea for the sketch? Well, Hormel also claims the honour of the world's first commercial radio jingle. You can hear it, as a UNIX .au format audio file, by going to their "SPAM in Time" page for the 1930s at *www.spam.com/it/it_30frame.htm*. You'll have to enable JavaScript to click on the link for the jingle, but the danger is almost worth it. Listen for yourself and see if you think there is a similarity between the jingle and the Viking's song ...)

spawning see *companion virus*

spear phishing *phishing* attacks targeted to a select group of individuals, usually within a company, rather than being *spammed* indiscriminately

spoofing attempt to gain access to a system by posing as an authorized user. Synonymous with impersonating, masquerading, or mimicking.

spyware type of *malware* that reports on the contents, status, or operation of the computer to a remote system or user. Generically, this could be almost any type of information gathering software. More specifically, it usually refers to modules or functions in software that report to the author, publisher, or service provider of an otherwise legitimate system. Spyware ranges from functions that report on version levels to the host system, through packages that report the presence of other software from the same manufacturer, through systems that gather information on all software installed including those from competing vendors, all the way to modules that report on the user's Web surfing. Justifications proposed for spyware include the need to ensure versions are kept up to date to provide proper service, concerns about software piracy, concerns about use for illegal or unacceptable purposes, and the gathering of marketing information. See also *adware*, *cookie*, and *web bug*.

standalone, shared system system that is physically and electrically isolated from all other systems, and is intended to be used by more than one person, either simultaneously (e.g., a system with multiple terminals) or serially, with data belonging to one user remaining available to the system while another user is using the system (e.g., a personal computer with nonremovable storage media such as a hard disk). U.S. government and military.

standalone, single-user system system that is physically and electrically isolated from all other systems, and is intended to be used by one person at a time, with no data belonging to other users remaining in the system (e.g., a personal computer with removable storage media such as a floppy disk). U.S. government and military.

standard part of the supporting detail of a security *policy*, a standard is a specific item of hardware or software, configuration, or level of performance that is to be adhered to in operations

star property see **-property*

State Delta Verification System system designed to give high confidence regarding microcode performance by using formulae that represent isolated states of a computation to check proofs concerning the course of that computation. U.S. government and military.

state variable variable that represents either the state of the system or the state of some system resource

stateful inspection form of *firewall* somewhat more advanced than a *screening router*, in which filtering is based on the contents of a sequence of *packets*, rather than a single packet

stealth various technologies used by viral programs to avoid detection on disk. At least one *virus* has been named "Stealth" by its author, but the term properly refers to the technology, and not a particular virus.

steganography activity of concealing a message by hiding the fact that communication is happening. Steganography is often referred to as "hiding in plain sight." Classical steganography systems depend on keeping the encoding system secret, but modern steganography is detectable only if secret information is known (e.g., a secret *key*). However, because of their invasive nature, most steganography systems leave detectable traces within a medium's characteristics. This allows an eavesdropper to detect media that has been modified, revealing that secret communication is taking place. Although the secrecy of the information is not degraded, its hidden nature may be revealed, defeating the main purpose of steganography.

stepanography writing a secret message on the back of a duck (per APP)

Stoned extremely successful MS-DOS *virus*, in terms of the number of copies made and systems infected. A *BSI* of *MBR* type, it has, like most successful viral programs, been used as a template for numerous other viral strains, including *Michelangelo.*

storage object *object* that supports both *read* and *write* *accesses*

stream cipher *cipher* that serially encrypts data, one bit at a time. Compare with *block cipher.*

subject active entity, generally in the form of a person, process, or device that causes information to flow among objects or changes the system state. Technically, a process/domain pair.

subject security level *subject's security level* is equal to the security level of the *objects* to which it has both *read* and *write access.* A subject's security level must always be dominated by the clearance of the user with which the subject is associated.

super-user user with full and unrestricted access to all aspects and resources of the system. Frequently referred to, particularly in UNIX circles where it is the name of the privileged account, as root, hence *root kit.*

supervisor state synonymous with *executive state*

surveillance systematic observation or monitoring of places, persons, or things by visual, aural, electronic, photographic, or other means

symmetric key encryption symmetric key *encryption*, otherwise known as private key encryption, uses the same, private, *key* for encryption and decryption, the key being shared between the two parties to the communication. Symmetric key systems do not require a *public key infrastructure*, as does *asymmetric* key encryption, but do require key exchange via a secure channel.

SYN flood *denial of service attack* that sends a host more TCP SYN *packets* (request to synchronize sequence numbers, used when opening a connection) than the protocol implementation can handle

system boot record on *ISA* or Wintel computers the first logical (not physical) *sector* of the master hard drive, or the first physical sector on a floppy diskette. The programming in the system boot record is called by the programming in the *master boot record* and points to the files needed to continue the boot process for the specific operating system being run. See also *boot record*, *boot sector*, and *master boot record*.

System Development Methodologies methodologies developed through software engineering to manage the complexity of system development. Development methodologies include software engineering aids and high-level design analysis tools.

system high security mode see *modes of operation*

system model collection of source code files, compilation and related tools, option and configuration information for the use of the tools, and instructions for the creation of a given application. A system model is similar to a *build*, although in modern application development it may be much more complex. A given development environment or CASE (Computer Aided Software Engineering) tool may be used to create the system model. As with building, testing must be applied to the correct system model, or it may give invalid results.

system virus *virus* that redirects system pointers and information to infect a file without actually changing the infected program file. This is a type of *stealth* technology. In MS-DOS, often referred to as a FAT or *cluster virus*. In Windows, system infectors usually make changes to the Windows Registry.

system integrity quality a system has when it performs its intended function in an unimpaired manner, free from deliberate or inadvertent unauthorized manipulation of the system

system low lowest security level supported by a system at a particular time or in a particular environment

System Security Officer (SSO) see *Information System Security Officer*

system virus sometimes used as a synonym for *cluster virus*, sometimes used to refer to a virus that makes changes to system structures such as the MS *Windows Registry* or program search paths

T

tampering unauthorized modification that alters the proper functioning of equipment or a system in a manner that degrades the security or functionality it provides

tarpit term is used for three slightly related means of delaying and disrupting unwanted behaviour. A group in Germany used the term "teergrube" to refer to a mail transfer agent that uses SMTP continuation lines to hold a mail connection open for long periods of time to disrupt *spamming* (www.iks-jena.de/mitarb/lutz/usenet/teergrube.en.html). The term is also used to describe throttling of the number of connections a computer can make to reduce the spread of *worms*. There is also a product that uses the term tarpit to refer to a single machine that emulates a large number of non-existent machines in a kind of *honeypot* configuration to provide delaying camouflage to divert an intruder.

TCB (Trusted Computing Base) the totality of protection mechanisms within a computer system, including hardware, firmware, and software, the combination of which is responsible for enforcing a *security policy*. A TCB consists of one or more components that together enforce a unified security policy over a product or system. The ability of a TCB to enforce correctly a unified security policy depends solely on the mechanisms within the TCB and on the correct input by system administrative personnel of parameters (e.g., a user's clearance level) related to the security policy. The term

"Trusted Computing Base" is now often applied to parts of Windows NT or 2000, regardless of certification or configuration, and Windows security literature usage in this regard is very confused between the operating system kernel, basic services running before user logon, and the Winlogon.exe program itself.

TCSEC see *DoD Trusted Computer System Evaluation Criteria*

technical attack attack that can be perpetrated by circumventing or nullifying hardware and software protection mechanisms, rather than by subverting system personnel or other users. Contrast with *social engineering*.

technical control see *controls*

technical vulnerability hardware, firmware, communication, or software flaw that leaves a computer processing system open for potential *exploitation*, either externally or internally, thereby resulting in *risk* for the owner, user, or manager of the system

TEMPEST study and control of spurious electronic signals emitted by electrical equipment, particularly in regard to the use of those emissions as a *covert channel*. I have been semi-reliably informed that, despite the capitalization, TEMPEST is not actually an acronym.

template file containing a Microsoft Word macro. Traditionally, templates are named with a .DOT extension, while documents have a .DOC extension, but either file can actually have any extension, or none. Technically, a Word document cannot contain a macro, but a template file can contain data. Therefore, .DOC files infected with *macro viruses* are templates, not documents. The user, of course, cannot tell the difference. (This technology modified with the release of Microsoft Office 2000.)

temporal isolation means of separating information and processing of information of differing levels of sensitivity by loading and processing data of such differing levels at different times. See also *periods processing*.

Terminal Access Controller Access Control System (TACACS) UDP (User Datagram Protocol) based authentication and *access control* protocol (RFC 1492) in which a network access server receives an identifier and password from a remote terminal and passes them to a separate *authentication* server for verification. TACACS uses centralized authentication servers and serves network access servers, routers, and other networked computing devices. TACACS+ is a TCP (Transmission Control Protocol) based protocol that improves on TACACS and XTACACS by separating the functions of authentication, *authorization*, and accounting and by encrypting all traffic between the network access server and authentication server. It is extensible to allow any authentication mechanism to be used with TACACS+ clients.

terminal identification means used to uniquely identify a terminal to a system

threat any circumstance or event with the potential to cause harm to a system in the form of destruction, disclosure, modification of data, and/or *denial of service*. Threat is the broadest category in a classification, becoming more specific as it moves through *vulnerability*, *exploit*, and *attack*.

threat agent method used to exploit a *vulnerability* in a system, operation, or facility, or an entity generating such an *exploit*

threat analysis examination of all actions and events that might adversely affect a system or operation

threat monitoring analysis, assessment, and review of audit trails and other data collected for the purpose of searching out system events that may constitute violations or attempted violations of system security. See also *intrusion detection system*.

three pillars three basic aspects of security are considered to be *confidentiality*, *integrity*, and *availability*, often referred to by the mnemonic CIA. As with almost any aspect of security, even the "three pillars" are subject to debate: some would say that there are only two (integrity is a "special case" of availability), while others argue for additional factors.

ticket-oriented computer protection system in which each *subject* maintains a list of unforgeable bit patterns, called tickets, one for each *object* the subject is authorized to *access*. Compare *list-oriented*.

time bomb sometimes used to refer to a *logic bomb* that *triggers* on a time event

time dependent password *password* that is valid only at a certain time of day or during a specified interval of time

TOAST acronym first used by Padgett Peterson to refer to *antiviral* software that makes extravagant claims, or where a company spends more on advertising than on development. The origin was a product that advertised itself as, "The Only Antivirus Software That Won't Be Obsolete By The Time You Finish Reading This Ad."

TOC/TOU (pronounced "talk to") a discrepancy between the time of a check being made, and the time the resource is used (Time Of Check versus Time Of Use). See *between-the-lines entry*, *hijacking*, and *piggy-back*.

token *authentication* tool, a device used to hold key or authentication values, or calculate, and possibly send and receive, responses to challenges during the user authentication process. Tokens may be small, hand-held hardware devices similar to pocket calculators or credit cards.

top-level specification nonprocedural description of system behaviour at the most abstract level; typically, a functional specification that omits all implementation details

TPE Trident Polymorphic Engine. Another version of the "mutation engine" type of function (see *MtE*) but done by a different group.

traffic analysis inference of information from observable characteristics of data flow(s), even when the data is encrypted or otherwise not directly available. Such

characteristics include the identities and locations of
the source(s) and destination(s), and the presence,
amount, frequency, and duration of occurrence. Also,
analysis of pizza deliveries to the Pentagon.

traffic padding generation of spurious instances of communication, spurious data units, and/or spurious
data within data units, intended to defeat traffic
analysis. (The CIA orders pizza even when nothing
is going on.)

tranquility security model rule stating that the *security level*
of an *object* cannot change while the object is being
processed by a system. Also, a state never achieved by
a security practitioner.

transponder transmitter that only operates having received
(and usually been powered by) a radio signal. Most
"contactless" identity cards are transponders.

trap door see *backdoor*

trigger in regard to *viruses* and other *malware*, most commonly refers to the event, or code waiting for an
event, that stimulates the activity of the *payload*. In
special cases, may also refer to the event or code that
causes reproduction or replication of the virus, if the
virus does not seek out suitable targets upon activation.

triple DES (3DES) any of a number of variations on the
DES block cipher symmetric algorithm. One of the
most widely used forms encrypts *plaintext* with one
key, decrypts the resulting *ciphertext* with a second
key (which, because the key is different, does not
actually decrypt the data but re-encrypts it in a

different way), and finally encrypts the result of the second operation with the first key again. Double DES, without the third phase, is subject to an *attack* known as *meet in the middle*, which attempts decryptions from both sides until a match appears. The pattern of encryption/decryption/encryption also provides for compatibility with single DES, if only one key is used.

trojan horse program that either pretends to have, or is described as having, a (beneficial) set of features but, either instead, or in addition, contains a damaging *payload*. Often, the functions surreptitiously exploit the legitimate *authorizations* of the invoking process or user to the detriment of security or integrity. The extent of the pretence and damage can vary widely. Most frequently, the usage is shortened to trojan. There is little agreement on whether the term should be capitalized, or how, but the most common usage tends to be "trojan horse" and "trojan," sometimes justified by the fact that the "Trojan Horse" should properly refer to what happened at Troy, although probably merely because techies do not like using the shift key if they don't have to. "Trojan" generally refers to a name brand of prophylactic.

trojanize to modify an existing program to include an unwanted or negative *payload*

trust extent to which one can have confidence that the system meets its objectives; that is, the system does what it claims to do and does not perform unwanted functions. This is in line with Gene Spafford's famous definition that a secure computer is one that does what it is supposed to.

Trust the Machines bumper sticker seen in Florida during and following the 2000 U.S. Presidential campaign, referring to the fact that the voting machines employed in the process used proprietary (and secret) programming, and had no verifiable audit trail. See *also GIGO*.

Trusted Computer System Evaluation Criteria see *DoD Trusted Computer System Evaluation Criteria*

trusted computer system system that employs sufficient hardware and software *assurance* measures to allow its use for simultaneous processing of a range of *sensitive* or *classified* information.

Trusted Computing Base see *TCB*

trusted distribution trusted method for distributing the *TCB* hardware, software, and firmware components, both originals and updates, that provides methods for protecting the TCB from modification during distribution and for detection of any changes to the TCB that may occur during distribution

trusted identification forwarding *identification* method used in networks whereby the sending host can verify that an authorized *user* on its system is attempting a connection to another host. The sending host transmits the required user *authentication* information to the receiving host. The receiving host can then verify that the user is validated for *access* to its system. This operation may be transparent to the user. See also *single sign-on* and *Kerberos*.

trusted path mechanism by which a person at a terminal can communicate directly with the *TCB*. This mechanism can only be activated by the person or the TCB and cannot be imitated by untrusted software.

trusted process process whose incorrect or malicious execution is capable of violating system *security policy*

trusted software software portion of the *TCB*

TSR "Terminate and Stay Resident." See *resident*.

tunnelling techniques that involve the tracing of the system interrupts to the final programming. Used by both *viral* and *antiviral* programs to detect or disable opposing programs.

tunnelling router router or system capable of routing traffic by encapsulating it for transmission across an untrusted network, or across a network using a different communications protocol. See also *virtual private network*.

two-factor authentication *authentication* based on at least two of the three major types of authentication: something a user knows, is, or has. To access a system, the user must demonstrate both factors.

U

untrusted process process that has not been evaluated or examined for adherence to the *security policy*. It may include incorrect or malicious code that attempts to circumvent the security mechanisms.

user person or process *accessing* a system by direct or indirect connections. Considered by many experts to be the entity responsible for the greatest range of security problems.

user ID unique symbol or character string that is used by a system to identify a specific *user*

user profile patterns of a user's activity that can be used to detect changes in normal routines

usual suspect the term is, as the saying has it, "known to the police," and is probably most famous from the 1942 version of *Casablanca*, in which Capt. Renault (Claude Rains) keeps repeating it. It has a particular meaning for those who are members of the CISSPforum mailing list, and is associated with mistakenly replying to mailing lists, rather than privately forwarding comments. However, it has greatest application in something of a warning during investigations. Concentrating, and sometimes fixating, on those we consider guilty can prejudice the inquiry, and, should we manage to convince ourselves that a "usual suspect" is guilty, we are at risk of letting the real culprit go free, and continue to attack. (In this regard, we come full circle back to *Casablanca*: Capt. Renault uses the phrase, at the end of the movie, to distract the chase from himself and Rick, played by Humphrey Bogart.)

V

vaccine program or code module that is attached, or attaches itself, to an executable program to perform a *change detection* check and warn if there have been any changes. Sometimes used as an *antiviral*, and sometimes simply to check for program corruption. The term "vaccine" is poorly defined, and infrequently used.

vampire data data the suspect in a case had thought dead, but was recovered in a *computer forensics* or *digital forensics* process to come back and bite them on the neck. (OK, it's slang, and it doesn't really have a meaning, but it's too cute to leave out.)

vampire tap means of tapping into coaxial (network) cable, by drilling through the layers of insulation and outer conductor, and attaching conductors to both the inner and outer conductors of the cable. This was actually the normal means of attaching connections to coaxial network cable. With the prevalence of twisted pair cabling, the technology is not used much any more. A similar operation can be performed on twisted pair cable, although the "vampire tap" term is generally not used in that regard.

variant modified version of a *virus*. Usually produced on purpose by the virus author or another person amending the virus code. If changes to the original are small, most antivirus products will also detect variants. However, if the changes are large, the variant may go undetected by anti-virus software.

verification process of comparing two levels of system specification for proper correspondence (e.g., *security policy model* with top-level specification, top-level specification with source code, or source code with object code). This process may or may not be automated.

viral having the features of a *virus*, particularly self-reproduction

virtual

If it's   there and you can   see it, it's real

If it's   there and you can't see it, it's transparent

If it's not there and you can   see it, it's virtual

If it's not there and you can't see it, it's **gone**

virtual memory memory as it appears to the operating programs running in the CPU; this memory may appear smaller, equal to, or larger than the real memory present in the system. Currently, the most frequent usage of the term is in regard to the practice of swapping or paging sections of physical memory to storage in disk, to make the memory space appear to be larger.

virtual private network (VPN) restricted-use, logical (that is, artificial or simulated) computer network that is constructed from the system resources of a relatively public, physical network (such as the Internet or the Public Switched Telephone Network—PSTN), often by using *encryption* (located at hosts or gateways), and often by *tunnelling* links of the virtual network across the real network. Note that a VPN has more to do with network management than *confidentiality*: encryption is not required for a VPN.

virus self-replicating and propagating program, usually operating with some form of input from the user, although generally the user is unaware of the intent of the virus. Often considered a self-propagating *trojan horse*, composed of a mission component, a *trigger* component, and a self-propagating component. A final definition has not yet been agreed upon by all researchers. A common definition is, "a program that modifies other programs to contain a possibly altered version of itself." This definition is generally attributed to Fred Cohen, although Dr. Cohen's actual definition is in mathematical form. Another possible definition is, "an entity that uses the resources of the host (system or computer) to reproduce itself and spread, without informed operator action."

virus hoax see *hoax*

vulnerability weakness in system security procedures, system design, implementation, internal controls, and so forth that could be exploited to violate system *security policy*; the possibility of an *exploit* or exposure to a *threat*, specific to a given platform

vulnerability analysis systematic examination of systems to determine the adequacy of security measures, identify security deficiencies, and provide data from which to predict the effectiveness of proposed security measures

vulnerability assessment measurement of *vulnerability* that includes the susceptibility of a particular system to a specific *attack* and the opportunities available to a *threat agent* to mount that attack

vx abbreviated reference to the "Virus eXchange" community; those people who consider it proper and right to write, share, and release *viral* programs, including those with damaging *payloads*. Originated by Sarah Gordon who has done extensive studies of the *virus* exchange and security breaking community and has an aversion to using the shift key.

W

wabbit (term almost certainly derived from Elmer Fudd's repeated line, "You wascawwy wabbit!" in the *Looney Tunes* cartoon series) mythical program reported, circa 1978, on a System/360 computer. The concept may have descended from a program called RABBITS reported from 1969 on a Burroughs 55000 at the University of Washington Computer Center. The program would allegedly make two copies of itself every time it was run, eventually crashing the system. (The existence of the two reported programs has not been confirmed.) See *rabbit*.

waiver permission to operate while not in compliance. Depending on who does the permitting, and what you aren't complying with, lawyers may salivate when this happens.

walk traversal of a data structure, especially an array or linked-list data structure in memory. In *forensic programming*, it is common to "walk the code" looking for modules, jumps, and operations: in *computer forensics*, frequently a utility will "walk the disk" checking for lost or apparently invalid pointers to data. (Walking the disk should not be confused with "walking drives," which was the practice of establishing a resonant frequency for moving [large] drive heads in old [large] disk drives, thus causing the drives to incrementally move across the floor.)

wannabe individual who "wants to be" accorded a higher status than he or she actually holds or rates.

Frequently seen in areas of the *blackhat* communities, where warez d00dz wannabe virus writers, virus writers wannabe script kiddiez, script kiddiez wannabe crackers, and crackers wannabe hackers.

warchalking similar to *wardriving*, warchalking generally involves walking around with a portable computer and wireless card. When a network is detected, a chalk mark is made on a wall or sidewalk indicating the existence of the network and the level of security. Despite the popularity of references to warchalking, the actual practice appears to be extremely limited. (Initially, in fact, the practice of warchalking was suggested for those wanting to make their own wireless network connections accessible to others.)

wardialling using a program to repeatedly dial numbers, usually in a sequential range, to determine which ones responded with modem tones. Generally of greater importance in the days when modems were the primary means of remote communications with computers. Modems are still generally left unsecured or poorly secured.

wardriving driving around an area (generally a business or light industrial area) with a portable computer (laptop or handheld) equipped with a wireless network card and detecting wireless network access points. Usually, wardriving systems are also equipped with GPS capability and software such as NetStumbler to determine security or *encryption* levels. A number of groups use collected information to produce maps showing accessible networks and their level of security.

warez cracked versions of commercial software from which copy protection has been removed. Those who do the stripping of copy protection are generally known as *crackers* or warez d00dz, although the "warez d00dz" term also refers to those who only trade pirated software.

warhead see *payload*

web bug link on a given Web page or embedded in an *email* message that contains a reference and connection to a different Web site and therefore, unknown to the user, passes a call, and information, to a remote site. Most commonly, a web bug is either invisible or unnoticeable (typically it is one pixel in size) in order not to alert the user to its presence. See also *adware, cookie,* and *spyware.*

web of trust *PKI* (Public Key Infrastructure) technique used in *PGP* for building a file of validated *public keys* by making personal judgments about being able to trust certain people to be properly vouching for the certified keys of other people

wild, in the see *in the wild*

Wild, In the (ItW) specific reference to those *viruses* formally mentioned in the WildList. The capitalization is in distinction to viruses found *in the wild* but not mentioned in the WildList.

Windows Registry database holding system startup, configuration, security, and file association information in Microsoft Windows 9*x*, Me, NT, and 2000 systems. This is the central repository of all such information, replacing the old CONFIG.SYS,

AUTOEXEC.BAT, and .INI files (although those files do still exist, and are sometimes used). The Registry is an enormous object, often holding megabytes of data, and difficult to search. It is now being used to start *viruses* at boot time, without placing the viruses in identifiable startup directories. Viruses affecting the Registry can be seen as system infectors, although changing the Registry is much easier than the programming the old MS-DOS system infectors had to use.

Windows Script Host (WSH) language similar to Visual Basic for Application (VBA) and Visual Basic Script (VBScript) that will run scripts on certain Windows systems. The *LoveLetter virus* was a Windows script virus and used WSH.

Wintel see *ISA*

whitehat in an attempt to avoid debates about "good" *hackers* versus "bad" hackers versus *crackers* versus phone *phreaks* versus virus writers versus *vxers*, the security community has taken to describing those who attempt to explore security solely from the perspective of defence as the "white hats." The term originates from old American western genre movies where the "good guys" always wore white hats. See also *blackhat*.

work-around means of avoiding a problem or security issue, usually by avoiding using the resource known to have a *vulnerability*. Work-arounds are usually temporary fixes. Over-reliance on work-arounds can be dangerous, as they are generally informal, undocumented, and may not be communicated to workers using the system subsequently.

work factor estimate of the effort or time needed by a potential penetrator with specified expertise and resources to overcome a protective measure. Often applied to *cryptanalysis*.

worm self-reproducing program that is distinguished from a *virus* by copying itself without being attached to a program file, or spreads over computer networks, particularly via email. Originally used (by John Shoch and Jon Hupp of the Xerox Palo Alto Research Center) to specify a distributed type of network program with many segments.

Worm "the" *worm*, the Internet/Morris/UNIX Worm of November 1988. See also *Code Red, Hybris, Interent Worm, latency, Loveletter, malware, Nimda,* and *tarpit.*

write fundamental operation that results only in the flow of information from a *subject* to an *object*

write access *permission* to *write* to an *object*

X

XOR exclusive OR. A Boolean operation that yields true
only if one of its operands is true and the other is
false. If both operands are the same (either true or
false), the operation yields false. Because the operation is bitwise, and reversed if performed twice with
the same operand, XOR is frequently used for
simple *encryption*, or as a part of encryption
processes.

Y

Y2K reference to the situation when the year changed from 1999 to 2000, and the concern that time-sensitive systems using two-digit year date fields would fail, or behave unpredictably, when that happened. Aside from the massive exercise in retrofitting systems, a major security concern was that the urgent redevelopment and patching of large numbers of systems would create loopholes and *vulnerabilities*. It should be noted that, due to the patching practice known as windowing, an unknown number of systems may still be vulnerable to failure as they reach the end of their windowing range.

Z

zero day originally, the term [certain period] *vulnerability* or *exploit* indicated relative ease of exploitation of vulnerabilities or activity on the part of the *blackhat* community: a "zero day" exploit was the theoretical limit of vulnerability. However, recently the media has used it in regard to software or video piracy, generic *antivirus* detection, reward programs for finding vulnerabilities, or even little known system vulnerabilities or dangerous practices. Therefore, the term has now been diluted to the point where it is unlikely to be a useful reference, and may engender confusion.

zerofill to fill unused storage locations with the value zero, or representation of the character denoting it. Also sometimes zeroize. See also *DEADBEEF*.

zine electronically distributed newsletter or magazine. The term is now widely used for all kinds of electronic journals, but initially referred to periodic compilations of security breaking techniques distributed by *blackhat* groups.

zombie specialized type of *backdoor* or remote access program designed as the agent, or client (middle layer) component of a *DDoS* (Distributed Denial of Service) network. Once a zombie is installed on a computer, it identifies itself to a master computer, and then waits for instructions from the master computer. Upon receipt of instructions from the master computer, a number of zombie machines will send attack *packets* to a target computer. Zombie may refer to the control program run to control one of the middle layer computers, or to a computer so controlled. See *also backdoor, DDoS,* and *RAT.*

zoo jargon reference to a set of *virus* programs of known characteristics used to test *antiviral* software

Appendix A

References

The terms included in this dictionary come from the vast field of security literature. There are, of course, works in any field that are more valuable or less so. I have, over a number of years, maintained a Web page for the use of CISSP candidates, citing recommended books in the particular domains of security. It is available at http://victoria.tc.ca/techrev/mnbksccd.htm (again, thanks to Gary and Mae Shearman).

In terms of breadth of scope, and currency of information, no single source can compare with the *Information Security Management Handbook* edited by Hal Tipton and Micki Krause. It is best to think of the ISMH not as a single book as such, since new editions and volumes come out regularly. Think of it as a fat, hardcover, expensive, but very valuable annual periodical.

I have noted other security dictionaries and glossaries in the Preface. There are additional dictionaries, in diverse fields of technology, which may be helpful. I've maintained a list of these at http://victoria.tc.ca/techrev/mnbkdc.htm.

As noted, communications has almost an embarrassment of riches in the number of dictionaries. Probably the most widely used and regarded is *Newton's Telecom Dictionary*, which has definitely been an inspiration for what I would like to do with this one. (Harry publishes new versions annually, and frequently more often.) Another valuable reference that straddles the encyclopedia/dictionary line is the *McGraw-Hill Encyclopedia of Networking and Telecommunications* by Tom Sheldon. The huge *Communications Standard Dictionary* by Martin H. Weik has an enormous number of entries, is good in engineering and the military, although it has gaps elsewhere, particularly in regard to the Internet and recent technologies. Julie Petersen's *Data and Telecommunications Dictionary* is particularly interesting as a historical and illustrative reference.

For general computer terminology, Mitchell Shnier's *Computer Dictionary* has certain holes, but is one of only two serious contenders. We are used to having Microsoft view the world in an isolated and idiosyncratic way, but the *Microsoft Press Computer Dictionary* is surprisingly careful and broadly based.

Then there are, well, "other" dictionaries. The ultimate is, of course, the *Jargon File* (use your favorite search engine to find the latest version online), which has been published by MIT Press as *The New Hacker's Dictionary*, and is an excellent introduction to hacker language and culture and society. (*The Jargon File* has been another major influence as I've been writing this dictionary.) *The Computer Contradictionary* by Stan Kelly-Bootle is a hilarious look at the jargon of the so-called "management" of information systems.

Appendix B

The Lagos Creeper Box

Stealing the Network: How to Own a Continent *is fiction (more a series of short stories or scenarios than a novel), but the authors intend the book to be taken as a serious addition to security literature. In Chapter 2 the technical aspects are fairly detailed and suitably realistic. (I can personally vouch for the fact that the description of the physical attributes of that specific hotel are bang on, although the ... umm ... social amenities are not.)*

As with any volume where multiple authors work on separate chapters, the quality of the writing varies. Overall, most of the book is readable as fiction, although it may not qualify as thriller level plotting.

This book is certainly interesting enough (albeit rather disjointed) as fiction, and technical enough for everyone tired of the usual Hollywood view of computers. The security risks noted are real, and therefore a read through the book could be used to alert non-specialists to a number of security issues and vulnerabilities. I enjoyed it and I think it's got a place in a careful security awareness program.—Rob Slade

Nigeria was a dump. Charlos now understood why nobody wanted to work there. It's Africa like you see it on CNN. And yet this was the country that had the largest oil reserve on the continent. Military rule for the past 30 years ensured that the money ended up mostly in some dictator's pocket and not on the streets where it belonged.

When Charlos got off the plane it was 00h30. The air was still sticky and hot, but unlike Miami, it smelled of rotten food. Charlos was used to it—it's the same smell you find in tropical regions like Kuala Lumpur, Brazil, and Jakarta. He has been to many such places, usually to perform the same type of function he was contracted to do here. He was tired, tired to the bone. The kind of tired that you get from sleeping too little for too long. How did he get himself in this rat hole of a place?

Laura19

It all started five years ago—he was working for an IT security development house, in charge of providing the glue between the developers and project management teams. As a side line "hobby" to keep the boredom at bay, he slowly became involved in the hacking scene—writing his own code, tinkering with code he copied from projects at work, hanging out in the right IRC channels, and participating on covert mailing lists. Life was peachy—with no real concern over who he annoyed with his hacking efforts, he owned systems on a regular basis.

The problems began when he read the mail of girl he met on IRC who called herself Laura19. She studied computer science at the University of Sussen; the same university where he studied electronic engineering. He had seen her on campus and from day one had a thing for her. He suspected that she disliked him, something that irritated him immensely. Having had access to the password file on one of the university's main UNIX machines, he put his machine to the task of cracking her password. It took a while, but after a couple of days Jack the Ripper struck gold - he had it. He proceeded to log in to the host with her password and page through her e-mail. It was seriously spicy—she was having relationships with two students at the same time and the e-mails they exchanged were hectically sexually charged. One night on IRC, Laura19 was dissing him in the public channel again. He had a couple of beers, was tired and depressed, and wasn't in the mood for getting his ego trampled on again. It was time for revenge. He opened her mailbox and started copy-and-pasting her mail to the public channel. After every paragraph he would add some cheesy comments.

In the end it was she who had the last laugh. The short version of events was this—Laura19 had a nervous breakdown. She also had very rich (and overly protective) parents. Her dad blamed her nervous breakdown (with good reason) on Charlos and his IRC session, and dragged him to court. The court threw out the case, but Charlos lost his job, and the local newspaper (where her mom worked) had a field day with the story. Now nobody would touch him—he applied for several jobs but as soon as potential employers recognized his name they would suddenly lose interest. To top it off his girlfriend read the newspaper article and promptly dumped him.

In those days he lived off the money he had accumulated during the previous years. He rented a small flat in a seedy part of town, ate junk food, drank black tea (his milk never lasted since he didn't have a fridge), and buried himself in his hobby. He cancelled his normal telephone line and his mobile phone contract because the only people he cared to talk to were online and not IRL. He lost interest in anything outside of his Internet connection. When his cash flow got tight he sold his TV and his car —he could walk to the McDonalds and supermarket. In real life he wasn't going anywhere. He told his family that he was working on a project for Microtech in the East, and mailed them every month from a hotmail address. When his friends (now quite worried) would come over to his flat he would pretend not to be there. Life continued like this for nearly 18 months. Then his cash ran out, the space heater ran out of diesel, and he caught bronchitis.

He was hospitalized and nearly died. When he recovered he had a huge amount of debt. He couldn't sell anything else simply because he didn't have anything else to sell. And there wasn't any money coming in. The turning point in his life came when he was asked by someone on IRC if he could "recover" a password. The person had a Microsoft Word file that was password protected and "lost" the password. Charlos normally would do it for free but he was pressed for cash and asked the person $350 to crack the password. To his total surprise the stranger agreed.

He used $50 for food and paid the rest to his debtors. It was the fastest $350 he made in last year and a half. And so it turned out that he registered a hushmail account and posted "will break any system—price negotiable" on all the mailing lists where he hung out. There was a flurry of responses, most of them copied to the mailing list, most of them people telling him how ridiculous he was. But two days later he received e-mail from a woman calling herself SuzieQ. The e-mail asked if he could obtain access to a mailbox. It was written in clear wording, and looked as if it was written by a person outside of the hacking scene. It also had a telephone number in the signature.

Charlos phoned the number from a payphone. When a woman answered the phone he asked for Suzie. "Suzie" said that she heard about his services from a friend; she offered $3000 if he could get access to a mailbox located at a little known ISP in Miami. She clearly wasn't technical—if he could get access to the mailbox, she wanted him to print out all the mail and fax it to her. Upon receiving the first page she would verify that it held valid content and wire half of the funds. After receiving the rest of the pages she would wire the rest. Charlos agreed—of course he agreed.

His friends at the telephone company told him that the fax number she gave him belonged to a company called FreeSpeak in Miami. Browsing the FreeSpeak Web site, Charlos found a Suzanne Conzales working in the HR department. The e-mail address he had received from Suzie was *antonio.c@lantic.com*. Her husband? Perhaps her brother or father? Looking it up, he found Atlantic was a small ISP with a shoddy Web site that seems to specialize in dial-up accounts. It was run by a crowd that was clearly not very security aware. Linked from the main page was a site where you could recover your dial-up password if you could answer some personal questions.

Charlos phoned Suzie, took a chance and asked her if she knew what her husband's mother's maiden name was. The shock and confusion in her voice told him that he was right; she was checking on her husband's e-mail account. After getting the necessary details from her he told her that she should get the wire transfer ready and keep the fax line open.

It was easy money, like shooting fish in a barrel. Charlos was totally amazed by the ignorance of "normal" people. He was amazed at how easily he could obtain information, mostly without any technical "l33tness." Life was getting better; he paid off his debt, was eating well again, and was doing ultimately exciting work. Life was peachy; that is, until Antonio Conzales's goons showed up one day on his doorstep and proceeded to knock him unconscious.

Events and timelines quickly blurred as he awoke to find himself on a yacht, looking up at the barrel of a 9mm pistol.

"So kid, you like spying on people?" the voice said above him.

Charlos' mind was rolling, trying to see through the fog of a concussion and blinding headache to the shadow of a man standing before him. He quickly tried to evaluate his situation. He didn't know where he was, or who held the gun, but he did know that the 9mm was moments from going off if he didn't do some talking.

"Listen, I don't know who you are, man."

"My name is Antonio Conzales, you hacked into my e-mail, and I don't take too kindly to that as you can see. Normally you would be dead already, but I wanted to make sure it was my wife that hired you and not anyone else."

It spun back to Charlos quickly. He tried to look past the muzzle of the gun to the man that was holding it. Making sure to steady his voice, he said,

"Yeah, just your wife, I don't know what you're about, I didn't see anything, I was just hired to deliver some information to her."

Charlos could see Antonio was more than just a little angry at him for breaking into his mailbox, and angry at his wife for hiring Charlos to do just that. Antonio seemed to be the type of guy who was very sensitive about his privacy, and as Charlos began to find out, he had good reason.

"Well, that's good to know." He said as the gun slowly lowered, "But I have a couple more questions I want to ask you before we decide what to do with you."

Antonio Conzales turned out to be into high tech, busty blondes, killing people and throwing them off his boat, and smuggling huge amounts of cocaine into America. The porn (featuring said busty blondes) that he was posting to various mailing lists in fact contained stego-encoded messages to his couriers throughout the country. Naturally paranoid when Charlos hacked into his business, he was also keen to pick up on a potential money-maker when he saw one. Antonio was a dirty player, but not stupid; he saw that Charlos had a talent that could be exploited and he was in a situation where he couldn't say no.

He grilled Charlos on the extent of his hacking capabilities before offering him an ultimatum. For having stuck his nose where it didn't belong, Charlos could either work for him, or "sleep with the fishes." For Charlos, the choice was simple: live another day.

Antonio became Charlos's agent after he consulted for him on his network security and set up an international network between various dealers, all communicated via images of naked women. Antonio quickly found himself in a new role as information broker, taking a 20 percent cut of his projects. With Antonio's extensive network of contacts, many in shady places, Charlos would get to do all the fun work and take 80 percent of the contract value.

Over the years Charlos got tired of the whole hacking scene—the geeks and nerds that call themselves hackers would spend months trying to bypass a firewall, get RAS credentials, or deliver a logic bomb via e-mail. He still had his hacking skill set but now his focus was more on getting the job done on time and less on the technical thrill of a perfectly cool hack. He found that hacking with real criminal intent was much more effective if you walk into a corporation with a suit and tie, sit down at an unoccupied cubicle, plug in a notebook, and walk out without a trace. And going physical always had that extra rush—he pushed the envelope to the point of having technical staff log him into their routers and security staff opening server closets.

Once inside he would map the network via SNMP (as most companies never set community strings on internal routers) and use his gentle asyncro portscanner to find boxes open on juicy ports such as 1433 (Microsoft SQL) or 139/445 (Microsoft RPC).

Using standard ARP cache poisoning he would try to sniff credentials going to POP3/IMAP servers, hashes of credentials to domain controllers, or even just good old Telnet passwords going in the clear. Most companies never patch their internal boxes; in his toolbox Charlos would have a bunch of industrial strength exploits. Armed with a network map, some credentials, and this toolbox he walked out of many large corporations with minutes of meetings, budget spreadsheets, confidential e-mails, and in the case of the job in Stockholm, even source code. Although such a semi-physical attack worked wonders, he still saw the merits in a methodical, covert approach. In fact, his current project started a month ago, back in the United States.

NOC NOC, Who's There?

The contract arrived from Antonio through the usual channels—a long-legged blonde with a tattoo of a spider on her hip. The job was a big one, and required traveling to Nigeria. The target was Paul Meyer, security officer for the NOC (Nigerian Oil Company), the largest exporter of crude oil in Nigeria. The assignment called for Charlos to obtain Meyer's credentials and a reliable channel to the NOC internal network. As a secondary objective, any information found on Meyer's hard drive was considered a bonus, which meant a bonus for Charlos. In other projects Charlos usually found out half-way through why the target was of importance: a political figure, the CFO of a company, a military leader, and so on. This one was straightforward; whoever employed him wanted unlimited access to NOC's network. Their motive for having access to NOC's network, however, was still a mystery.

As usual, Charlos started his project by Googling for Paul Meyer. Meyer appeared to be a South African contractor working in Nigeria for NOC. He was part of SALUG, the South African Linux user group. He made several posts about kernel modifications and firewall rule base management. From his posts Charlos figured that Meyer was no dummy, and more important, security aware. Meyer also made some posts from his NOC e-mail address. These were more subdued; he clearly didn't want to give away too much about the infrastructure or technologies of NOC. Meyer appeared to be an online-type person, like most good security officers; he frequently made posts, was quoted on chat rooms, and even had his own homepage. This was all good news for Charlos—the more he could learn from his target, the better.

Owning Meyer online clearly would not work. From his posts Charlos could deduce that the man probably could not be conned into running a Trojan, had his personal machine neatly firewalled, and took care to install the most recent service packs. He also figured that Meyer's PC was running a particular flavor of UNIX. Charlos wondered if his employers went down the same route, that NOC itself was a heavily fortified network and that they couldn't get to Meyer in the usual ways. Perhaps they hit a brick wall trying to get into NOC from the Internet, then targeted Meyer only to find out that he couldn't be taken. Which would explain why he was contacted—to go do the meat thing in Nigeria. Though Antonio usually provided interesting work it seldom required an elegant hack.

A big break for Charlos was finding out that Paul Meyer used MSN, probably to communicate with his friends and family back in South Africa. MSN's search function had proved to be a good source of intelligence before. If he could convince Meyer to add him as a contact he could possibly find a pattern in his online behavior, maybe even social engineer some details of the NOC network. Charlos started looking for people that Meyer spoke to in his online capacity. Jacob Verhoef was one of these people. Meyer frequently responded to Verhoef's posts, and some additional Googling proved that these two studied together. He created the e-mail address with as much detail as possible, to convince Meyer it belonged to his friend Jacob, hoping that Meyer automatically would assume it was the real Verhoef. What were the chances that Meyer and Verhoef have been talking online already? It was a chance he had to take. Charlos registered a hotmail account: jacob.verhoef1@hotmail.com. He filled in all the registration forms as accurately as possible.

It worked—Meyer allowed him to be added as a contact and "Jacob Verhoef" had some interesting chats with him. Whenever Meyer starting referring to their varsity days, "Verhoef" became vague and switched his status to offline, blaming South African Telkom for their poor service when he went back online. A bigger challenge (that Charlos never thought about) was the language; it turned out that both Meyer and Verhoef spoke Afrikaans. When Meyer typed in Afrikaans, Charlos would always respond in English, and soon Meyer would follow suit. They didn't speak too much; whenever Charlos steered the conversation to the NOC's network, Meyer just sidestepped it. But this was enough for Charlos—he could monitor exactly when Meyer was at work and at home. His target followed a strict routine—his status changed from Away to Online from about 7h00 in the morning, there was a break from about 7h50 to 8h30 (while he was traveling to work, which, thanks to traffic in Lagos was typically a long commute), he stayed online most of the day until exactly 17h00, and then would head back home, being online from 20h00 to around midnight. Weekends were different, with no apparent pattern.

And so he found himself at passport control at Lagos International Airport. He was there as a computer forensic expert working on a case for the First Standard National Bank of Nigeria (SNBN)—though SNBN did not really exist. Having traded some personal details of wealthy business men in Lisbon (which was "bonus" material from another project) with a group of 419 scammers he now had all the right papers. Charlos knew that sticking close to the story was essential. If they opened his notebook bag and found his equipment it would be difficult to explain; that is, unless he was a computer forensic expert on a job for SNBN.

He took a taxi to Hotel Le Meridian. Everything in Lagos was dirty and broken. Even with its four stars and a price tag of $300 per night, the hotel's water had the same color as Dr. Pepper. You couldn't even brush your teeth in this water let alone drink it. He went down to the bar area, and had a Star Beer and chili chicken pizza. It was not long before the prostitutes hanging around made their way to him. He was blunt but polite with them—he was in no mood for a dose of exotic STDs, and besides, he had work to do the next morning.

Lagos is rotten with wireless communication systems—satellite, WiFi, microwave—you name it. Since the decay of public services, the only way to communicate fairly reliably with the outside was via wireless systems. Charlos decided to take a cab to the NOC's compound—every taxi driver knows the exact location of these compounds. The compounds are the retreats for foreign nationals working in Lagos—the only way that a company can get contractors to work for them is to place them securely in a compound. There they have access to running water, Internet connectivity, personal drivers, and internal canteens. "It's a bit like an internal network," Charlos thought. Once inside the gates of the compound you are trusted, especially if you are white and have a foreign accent.

Once inside the taxi he booted his notebook and started NetStumbler. Along the way to the compound Charlos stumbled across many networks, most of them without any type of encryption. He asked the driver how far away they were from the NOC compound. When they were about ten minutes from the compound, Charlos told the driver to stop. He was DHCP-ed into the internal network of a bank, with unhindered access to the Internet. He logged into MSN as Jacob Verhoef. Meyer was logged in. It was 10 A.M.—chances were good that he was at work. He told the driver to continue.

Doing the Meat Thing

Security at the main gate of the compound was probably as good as physical security could be in Nigeria—a guard armed with an AK47 and a logbook in a hut. As the taxi stopped, Charlos rolled down his window. Charlos was dressed in a white flannel shirt, dark brown pants, and sandals. He hid the notebook under the seat and smiled at the security guard. "Hi, my name is Robert Redford. I came here to visit Paul Meyer; he works for the NOC."

"Did you make an appointment?"

Charlos didn't expect this but kept his cool. "I am in Lagos for business. Paul is an old friend of mine; we used to study together..."

"Sorry sir, without an appointment you cannot pass."

Charlos reached for his pocket and pulled out a couple of 100 Naira bills. "Please," he said, holding out the notes, "I am only here today. Tomorrow I fly back again." The guard eagerly took the money. "Do you know which room I could find him?" Charlos pushed his luck. But the guard did not know and Charlos's taxi rolled into the compound.

He walked toward what appeared to be the entertainment area—a big screen TV tuned to some sports channel was situated in the corner. There was a Sony PlayStation II hooked up to the TV and a stack of pirated DVDs lying on a coffee table. On the couch a man was sleeping; his forehead was covered in sweat and Charlos figured he was sweating out a malaria attack. Charlos woke him up. "Do you know where I can find Paul Meyer?"

"He's not here, he's at work, where else?!" the man grunted. He spoke with a thick Australian accent and it was clear that he was in pain and annoyed that someone woke him from his feverish dreams.

Charlos pushed on, "I'm an old friend of his, he said to meet me here at 10:30."

"Room 216, west wing."

The door at Meyer's flat was locked, and there was no key-hole—a numeric keypad was installed. Probably because of the high volume of contractors that stay for only a month, pack up their stuff and leave at night, Charlos thought. Charlos was feeling a bit disappointed that he never asked Meyer about access to his room. He slipped with that little detail. His lock picking equipment was rendered useless. He tried 1234 as a PIN; it didn't work. He tried 0000; it didn't work either. Charlos remembered from his research that Meyer's birthday was the 14th of May and he was 31 years old. He remembered it because Meyer shared his birthday with Charlos's ex-wife. He tried 1405; no luck. 0514 didn't work. Finally, Charlos tried 1973 and he could hear the door click open. He was lucky this time.

Once inside the room Charlos was in known territory. He gently closed the door behind him, put on his surgical gloves, and took out his palm-sized digital camera. He took a few pictures of the room. This served two purposes: to ensure he left everything exactly the way it was when he walked into the room, and as additional proof to his employers that he had indeed reached his target. The place was a mess of computer equipment; Charlos smiled. The less organized, the less chance of Meyer finding anything out of place. Meyer's flat had a double bed, a walk-in kitchenette, bathroom, and living area. The living area had been transformed into an office/lab environment. There were several Ethernet cables hanging from the table, WiFi APs, computers without their covers, and audio equipment. These were decorated with coffee mugs, empty soft drink cans, and snubbed out cigarette butts—one or two days' worth, not more. "My kind of place," Charlos muttered. He picked up the telephone in Meyer's room and phoned his prepaid cell phone (it was a habit of his to get his target's phone number). Charlos started looking around for Meyer's main computer. In the center of the table were two 17" flat panels, an optical trackball mouse, and a keyboard. No computer. A Sun Sparc 10 sat perched on the floor, without a screen, but with a keyboard on top of it. Then he saw it—a Dell docking station attached to the main keyboard, and a clear open space on the table where the notebook must be. Meyer apparently took his notebook with him to work and brought it back here. This meant complications for Charlos. He could bug the keyboard here in the flat, but it meant missing out on his bonus, the files on Meyer's machine. Did Meyer even connect to the NOC network from home? Would he be able to steal credentials to the NOC network from here? Charlos started by installing the keystroke logger first.

He gently opened the keyboard with his electric screwdriver. When you've done this hundreds of times it becomes second nature. The keyboard's coiled wire plugged into the keyboard via a small white clip. The keyboard logger chip that Charlos used had two white clips on it, a male and a female. The chip clips in where the keyboard normally plugs in, and the coiled cabled plugs into the chip. Finally, the chip secures neatly to the keyboard's plastic cover with some double-sided tape. Keyboard logger manufacturers quickly discovered that the speed at which a device can be commissioned was a major selling point. Gone were the days of cutting wires and struggling with a soldering iron.

Charlos put the beige-colored keyboard cover back on and shook the keyboard. No rattles, no loose keys, as good as new. Nobody would ever think the device was bugged. He plugged the keyboard back into the docking station. In a sense he was lucky—he didn't have to take any chances with plugging out the keyboard on a live machine. This sometimes required a reboot of the machine—not a big problem in Nigeria with its unreliable power supply.

He looked at his watch: 11h36. He still had plenty of time to install the creeper box. The creeper box was worth its weight in gold. A very small PC with a footprint of about 12x12x4 cm, equipped with a single Ethernet and tri-band GSM modem, the creeper could be installed virtually anywhere there was power, GSM coverage, and Ethernet. Whatever the assignment, Charlos always packed a creeper box. Once installed, the creeper would periodically dial out via GPRS to the Internet, making it a box that can be controlled from anywhere in the world. As soon as the machine connected to the Internet it would SMS him its IP number, a machine on the internal network totally under his control. The box packed all the latest exploits, tools needed to sniff the network, inject packets, and scanners. It could be remotely booted into a choice of either Linux or XP.

Charlos booted his notebook. The idea was to plug into the hub and get a sense of the traffic that was floating on the network in order to assign the creeper an IP address on Meyer's internal network. But something strange happened. With his notebook booted into Windows XP it registered a wireless network. The SSID of the network name was NOCCOMP—the NOC compound. A DHCP server already assigned an IP address to his notebook. No WEP, nothing. Charlos smiled. In fact, he laughed out loud, added an "ipconfig /all", and noted the IP number.

The question now was, how deep in the NOC network was this compound wireless network? Charlos dialed into the Internet from his GSM phone, and tried a zone transfer of the noc.co.ng domain. It was refused. He ran his DNS brute forcer and within five minutes saw that the server intranet-1.noc.co.ng had an IP address of 172.16.0.7. The IP given to him by the compound's DHCP server was in the 10 range. Both IP numbers were assigned to internal networks, but that meant nothing. The networks could be totally separate or maybe filtered by a nasty firewall. Charlos terminated his call and reconnected to the wireless network. Again he received an IP address in the 10 range. His fingers trembled as he entered "ping 172.16.0.7". And voilà, it responded less than 100ms. Not local, but not far away. Now for the major test: A quick portscan would reveal if the machine was indeed filtered. Charlos whipped up an Nmap. The results came in fast and furious: 21,80,139,443,445,1433. Default state: closed. This meant that the server was totally open from his IP—no filtering or firewalling was done. Charlos was tempted to take a further look at the wide-open network, but thought otherwise. He was contracted to get Meyer's credentials and create a channel into the NOC network.

From his bag of tricks Charlos took a PCMCIA cradle and unscrewed the Ethernet card from the creeper. Who needs to hook into Meyer's network if you have unhindered access to the NOC internal network via the wireless network? He slid one of his 802.11b cards into the cradle and closed the creeper again. This was just beautiful—he had GSM on the one interface, WiFi on the other—all he needed was power. He didn't even have to place the box in Meyer's room; it could be anywhere in the compound! Meyer's room was as good as any place; he would probably notice the device only when he moved out of his flat. Charlos started looking around for a good hiding place for the machine. With trouble he moved the 2m high bookcase away from the wall. He was indeed lucky. Behind the bookcase was a power outlet. He gave the creeper power and set it down on top of the bookcase. He moved the case back against the wall, and started walking around in the room, making sure the box was not visible from any point in the flat. While still doing so his cell phone vibrated inside his pocket—it was the creeper reporting in over the Internet.

Before leaving the apartment, Charlos checked the pictures on his digital camera. He moved the keyboard a few inches to the left, not that he thought Meyer would ever notice, but he took pride in his work. Everything had to be perfect. He checked his watch: 12h44. He was hungry. His taxi was still waiting for him in the parking lot. He was in time to get a Star and a chili chicken pizza at the hotel for lunch.

Back at the hotel, Charlos had lunch and a quick nap; the jet lag still hadn't worn off. By the time he woke up it was 16h55 and he had another SMS from his creeper box, faithfully checking in every four hours and disconnecting from the Internet after five minutes of inactivity. His next window was at around 20h40. He should check that everything is in place. He hung around the hotel for the next couple of hours taking a swim, going to the gym, smoking a couple of cigarettes, watching CNN. Just after eight, Charlos dialed up to the Internet from his GSM phone. From his · MSN window Charlos would see that Meyer was online. At 20h38 his phone signaled the awakening of the creeper again. He SSH-ed into the box on port 9022, configured the wireless interface, and received an IP address from the compound's DHCP server. There was significant lag on the line, but that was just because of his slow 9600 baud connection. It was time to conclude his little project.

Charlos fired up Tethereal on the creeper. He could see a lot of traffic floating over the wireless network—mostly HTTP requests to porn sites, MSN, e-mail, and some IRC. He entered into conversation with Paul Meyer. The idea was to see if he could see Meyer's traffic. Was Meyer's little "home" network connected to the NOC's compound network via the same wireless network? It was indeed. As "Jacob Verhoef" chatted to Paul Meyer, Charlos could see the conversation on his creeper's sniffer. Charlos remembered the APs he saw in Paul's place. This was good, really good. Although Charlos didn't own Meyer's machine it felt like he did. Now all he had to do was get him to log into the NOC domain, perhaps some firewalls, a router here, a fileserver there. Although most of the protocols are encrypted, his keystroke recorder would record every keystroke, including usernames, passwords, and so on.

It didn't happen that night or the night after that. Charlos was getting totally sick of Stars, chili chicken pizza, playing pool at the bar, and keeping the prostitutes at bay. His patience was running out fast. He had credentials as domain controller to the NOC domain, Meyer's personal mailbox, his MSN account, and more, but he lacked credentials to the firewalls and routers. Four days after he planted the bugs he made a bold move—he faked a CERT advisory to the "Full Disclosure" mailing list stating that a terrible virus is sweeping across the world using IP protocol 82 and 89. All Cisco routers should be patched, and administrators must make sure they block these protocols on their firewalls. Charlos sent the advisory at around 8:00, making sure that Meyer would receive the alert while at home. It proved to be very effective. As a good security officer Meyer was logging into every router and firewall in the NOC network, blocking these protocols with ACLs on the routers and packet filters on the firewalls.

Charlos gave his logger another week - it had the capacity for half a million keystrokes and he was starting to ease into a routine at the hotel. Full disclosure discredited the CERT advisory. It became just another topic of pointless discussion, but it served its purpose. Two weeks since he arrived in Lagos, Charlos paid Meyer's room another visit. Knowing the combination to his room and using his "only here for a day" excuse with the gate guard Charlos slipped into Paul Meyer's room, removed the chip from his keyboard, and headed back to the hotel. He put the chip into a plastic bag, along with the chip's password. In another bag he inserted the GSM SIM card, the SIM card's PIN, and instructions on the schedule of the creeper plus how to connect to it over the Internet. He added some of the photos he took of Meyer's room to the bag. Finally, he made a list of passwords and IP numbers he obtained from the chip on a single piece of paper. All this was inserted into a small wooden box, wrapped in heavy duty brown paper. He made sure he wiped his fingerprints from the bag and the package—you can never be too sure. On his way to the airport Charlos stopped at DHL offices and mailed the package to the address given to him by Antonio. The name on the address was just "Knuth," no last name or first name. That seemed a little odd to Charlos, but as he had found out, curiosity could get him killed, so he just moved forward with what he was hired to do. He wiped the prepaid cell phone clean of any fingerprints and dropped it with the SIM card intact into the river.

And just like that… he disappeared.

To read more, visit www.syngress.com.

Printed and bound by CPI Group (UK) Ltd, Croydon, CR0 4YY

03/10/2024

01040437-0004